BLACK
BUILT

BLACK BUILT

BUILT

History and Architecture
in the Black Community

Paul Wellington

For Mazie, Violet, and lovers of architecture, history, and the Black community.

CONTENTS

INTRODUCTION

Of the 113,000 architects in the United States, only two percent identify as Black. Representation in the field is severely disproportionate, as Blacks account for more than thirteen percent of the nation's population. Many factors have contributed to the profession's lack of diversity, stemming from cultural and economic forces, as well as general lack of awareness. For many impressionable Black youth, their experience with architects is virtually nonexistent. Within urban neighborhoods, their role models are formed from environmental interests, resulting in music, sport, and fashion aspirations. The lack of additional career choices is, in part, an effect of inadequate school funding. Art, music, technology, and hands-on classes have the ability to instill creativity and self-expression in young minds. Without these foundations, careers such as architecture are not often considered, contributing to the profession's lack of Black architects.

Architecture's lack of Black professionals stems from the Harlem Renaissance in the 1920s, a period of significant Black cultural activity. Though the movement produced advances in intellectual, social, and artistic development, architecture failed to gain traction. Black architects were concerned with keeping up with their White counterparts rather than advocating a Black aesthetic. The effects of that failed connection have lasted well into the 21st century, as growth has been marginal. In addition, many Blacks gravitate towards careers high in social value (e.g. teaching, nursing, social work, etc.), as a means of giving back to low-income communities. Architecture does not immediately provide this value and suffers in the recruitment of Black talent.

Though there is a lack of Black architects, many have designed remarkable buildings and projects. Their works cover a wide variety of place types, including museums, churches, homes, and businesses. Many of these works are found in Black communities, providing opportunities for Black youth to gain an appreciation for architecture; however, how are they found? It is generally impossible for the average person to recognize the architects of buildings, as most places seamlessly integrate into their surroundings, failing to reveal their history.

This book uncovers the works of Black architects, encompassing a wide variety of projects that showcase both their talents and the impact of their work in the Black community. The works highlighted span from the 19th century to present and cover a variety of cities from across the United States. Each entry discusses the history of a project, its architecture, and selected achievements. While not every architect discussed in this book is on a building's official record, their influence and expertise assisted in a project's acquisition, design, and completion.

Architecture functions as one of the most important aspects of human culture. It is one of the few remnants of past civilizations, and it defines how people live, socialize, and visualize their environment. Few Black architects have had the opportunity to define an environment, and little is known of their works outside of the architecture profession. This book serves as an introduction to their work, as well as an inspiration to a new generation of Black architects and communities.

1

ADAM CLAYTON POWELL JR. STATE OFFICE BUILDING

PERCY C. IFILL, CONRAD JOHNSON JR., GEORGE HANCHARD *(Ifill Johnson Hanchard)*
New York City, NY (1973)

The Adam Clayton Powell Jr. State Office Building stands as the tallest building in Harlem. Though brutalist in style, the high-rise reflects the heritage of its community, through its abstract design of an African mask. The building originally opened as the Harlem State Office Building, however in 1974 it was renamed in honor of Adam Clayton Powell Jr., New York's first Black member of the House of Representatives. A statue in his likeness resides in the front plaza, portraying Powell ascending a hill, representing his journey for equality and justice for African Americans.

Governor Nelson Rockefeller first conceived the idea of a state office building in Harlem in 1966. The governor hoped to occupy a more significant state presence in the predominantly Black community and enlisted the prestigious architects Phillip Johnson and John Burgee for a prominent location. Their design featured a complex surrounding an internal pedestrian plaza; however, political and racial pressure forced the architects to withdraw their services. The Black firm of Ifill Johnson Hanchard quickly replaced the original architects and devised a 24-story tower set away from a public plaza. The plan received harsh criticism, as residents desired low-income housing, a cultural center, and a school to unite the community. Opposition even went to such lengths as to stage a 'squat-in' in apartments, yet Rockefeller continued the project through the demolition of the site's buildings. Tensions remained high during the construction phase, as protests over the racial makeup of construction workers halted progress.

Topping out at 19 stories, the Adam Clayton Powell Jr. State Office Building opened proud, yet removed from its surroundings. The structure rests on a recessed base, giving way to cantilevered glass volumes attached by massive concrete pillars. The building provides the community the chance to embrace its presence, allowing a sense of control over political affairs. Despite its intention, the building has received unfavorable reviews, including from renowned architecture critic Paul Goldberger, who deemed the structure mediocre. Only within the past decade has a revitalization taken place, including the opening of restaurants, shops, and high-rise apartments in Harlem.

ADAM'S MARK HOTEL

HALEVY SIMMONS *(HBE Corporation)*
St. Louis, MO (1986)

Once part of a prestigious chain, the Adam's Mark Hotel originally stood as the Pierce Building in downtown St. Louis. Completed in 1907, the building was described as the largest building west of the Mississippi River. It was also credited with continuing the city's financial district as many businesses ventured west during the early 20th century. The Pierce Building's architect, Frederick C. Bonsak, was directly influenced by the Chicago School architectural style, and many of its characteristics were demonstrated in the building's original design. Piers running the height of the facade emphasized verticality, while vast expanses of glass provided ample natural light. The building also featured a clear tripartite design, with a prominent base, body, and crown.

Over the decades, the Pierce Building fell out of favor with the city, particularly after the opening of the adjacent Gateway Arch in 1965. Nearly twenty years later, the HBE Corporation purchased the site and opened the Adam's Mark Hotel. The original building was stripped down to its base structure, expanded with two eastern wings, and reclad in a brick veneer. Fred Kummer, CEO and owner of HBE, specifically hired architect Halevy Simmons due to their shared strong will and passion for design. Kummer's desire to reuse the Pierce Building, as opposed to deconstruction, presented a tall challenge for any architect, one embraced and achieved by Simmons.

In 2008, the Adam's Mark Hotel was sold and rebranded as a Hyatt Regency. The rebranding transpired one year after the chain's hotels were sold to Chartres Lodging Group. Ironically, despite Simmons's previous work with the hotel, the chain faced numerous allegations of racial inequality against African Americans. Such occurrences included non-promotions to management positions and the hanging of a slave doll, mocking the death of Sandra Bland. Despite the Adam's Mark Hotel's demise, the once prosperous chain has left its legacy across St. Louis. The hotel remains one of the city's most famed buildings, as well as one of the premiere buildings ever designed by a Black architect.

AFRICAN AMERICAN CIVIL WAR MEMORIAL

PAUL S. DEVROUAX and MARSHALL PURNELL *(Devrouax & Purnell Architects)*

Washington D.C. (1998)

The African American Civil War Memorial commemorates the contributions of Black soldiers who fought alongside the Union in the Civil War. The Spirit of Freedom, the centerpiece sculpture depicting Black troops and a family, was designed by renowned African American sculptor Ed Hamilton. Surrounding the sculpture is the Wall of Honor, listing the names of 209,145 United States Colored Troops (USCT) who served during the war. The memorial stands in proximity to Howard University and was the first national memorial placed in a Washington D.C. neighborhood, as opposed to the National Mall.

Adjacent to the memorial is the accompanying African American Civil War Foundation and Museum. The foundation was organized in 1992 to give voice to USCT and revitalize the community devastated by the 1968 riots. Its mission is to "serve the educational needs of its local, national and international community[1]" by interpreting the lives and legacy of USCT before, during, and after the Civil War. Under strong leadership, the museum opened in 1999 and relocated to its present location of the Grimke Building in 2011. The new site was chosen in part for its name, as it honors the slave-born Archibald Grimke, recognized as the second Black graduate of Harvard Law School and an advocate of education, civil rights, religion, and the arts.

The museum offers a multitude of resources that tell the story of USCT. Displays of photographs, articles, uniforms, and weaponry provide an in-depth visual reminder of the Civil War. Programs, events, performances, and the USCT registry also provide additional education and understanding. The success of both the museum and memorial is not limited to their shared wall and boundaries. Together, they have played a significant role in their community's revitalization as a central hub for artistic culture.

---

[1] "Memorial & Museum History." (p.101)

AFRICAN AMERICAN LIBRARY AND MUSEUM AT THE GREGORY SCHOOL

TERRY D. SMITH *(Smith & Company Architects)*

Houston, TX (renovation 2009)

While the African American Library and Museum at the Gregory School opened in 2009, the history of its presence dates back to 1870. Previous schools in churches provided primary education to the residents of Freedman's Town; however, the actions of the Texas legislature led to the founding of the Edgar M. Gregory Institute, one of the earliest public schools for African Americans in Texas. The 20,000 square foot school, named after a Union officer, settled in its current location in 1926, where it remained successful until 1984, when low enrollment forced its closure.

Freedman's Town was formed by 1,000 freed slaves after the Civil War. Its African American residents remained segregated from nearby communities, as White residents refused to intermingle. The location was selected primarily for its affordable land, a flood-prone swamp at the edge of a bayou. As an independent community, the town grew rapidly and remained sustainable by constructing schools, churches, and businesses. By 1930, Freedman's Town grew into the heart of Houston's Black culture, boasting jazz clubs and restaurants, which attracted residents from across the city. In the 1930s and 40s, the community was displaced by the expansion of nearby downtown, a freeway, and the San Felipe Courts housing project (an all White community until 1968). Further developments nearly removed all remnants of Freedman's Town, until historic preservations pushed for a historical designation in the 1970s. A national register historic site designation was granted in 1985, serving as the catalyst for increased preservation and thoughtful redevelopment efforts.

As part of Freedman's Town's revitalization, the Gregory School reopened as a library and museum after more than twenty years of abandonment. The first floor houses exhibits dedicated to the African American experience. The second level is home to a reading room, library, and research spaces. Weathered windows and bricks were restored to their original appearance and luster. Additionally, interior details, such as unfinished concrete floors and wooden handrails, transformed the space back to its original 1926 design. Upon entering the building, visitors pass through a transparent 2,000 square foot lobby, framed against the original structure, signifying the facility's mix of contemporary and historic architecture. With its comprehensive collection of regional African American knowledge, the African American Library and Museum at the Gregory School is one of the few libraries of its kind in the United States.

Selected Accolades: LEED Gold, Renovation/Restoration Design Award - Houston AIA (2010), Historic Rehabilitation Honor Award - Preservation Texas (2011), Good Brick Award - Greater Houston Preservation Alliance (2011)

AFRICAN BURIAL GROUND
NATIONAL MONUMENT AND VISITOR CENTER

Monument - NICOLE HOLLANT-DENIS and RODNEY LEON *(AARRIS Architects)*
Visitor Center - ROBERTA WASHINGTON *(Roberta Washington Architects), Amaze Design*
New York City, NY (2007 & 2010)

The construction of the US General Services Administration's (GSA) new Ted Weiss Federal Building in 1991 led to the discovery of hundreds of African American remains. Construction immediately halted, and archaeologists were able to uncover 419 skeletons and artifacts from the burial site. The site and its surrounding area in lower Manhattan contained the remains of nearly 20,000 slaves and freedmen, dating back to the 17th and 18th centuries. Though many bodies remain under the foundations of Manhattan high-rises, the accidental discovery at GSA's site provides a glimpse into a past Black culture and experience.

The magnitude of the discovery prompted the call for a meaningful memorial, leading to 61 applicants submitting a proposal in 1998. Rodney Leon, a local Black architect, submitted the winning project exhibiting the historical and cultural reverence of the site. Rising 24 feet above street level is the Ancestral Chamber, a transitional passageway into the sacred memorial. The site is also accessed by the Spiral Processional Ramp, which descends six feet below street level to evoke a deep connection to the burial grounds.

For seven years after the discovery, scholars from Howard University thoroughly analyzed the bones and relics. The remains were carefully memorialized in 2003, and themes from the findings became the guiding discussions during the development of the new 3,000 square foot visitor center. Located adjacent to the memorial in the Ted Weiss Federal Building is the visitor center, whose static and visual displays reclaim, examine, and preserve the site's history. Inside, visitors traverse through glimpses of past African American lives and learn the harsh realities faced by slaves on a daily basis. Along with the memorial, the visitor center serves as a much needed landmark in Lower Manhattan. Both Black slaves and freed persons were an integral part of New York's storied history, and their legacy deserves to be presented and preserved for generations to come.

Selected Accolades: National Historic Landmark (1993), National Monument (2006), Presidential Award - Preserve America (2008)

AUGUST WILSON CENTER FOR AFRICAN AMERICAN CULTURE

ALLISON WILLIAMS *(Perkins + Will)*

Pittsburgh, PA (2009)

The August Wilson Center (AWC) for African American Culture celebrates Pittsburgh's African American community. The prominence of the city's Black culture stems from the 1920s, during a prolific era of talented musical, visual, and performing artists. Community leaders advocated for a dedicated space to showcase the vibrant scene; however, a permanent location proved challenging to acquire. Noble attempts by the Homewood Art Museum and Carnegie Museum of Art failed to obtain adequate funding and truly define a space for the celebration of African American culture.

In 1996, land in the downtown district was approved for the building of a permanent African American center. A debate sparked over the center's location, with the predominantly Black Hill District given consideration; however, downtown's central location was justified as an attraction for all Pittsburgh residents. AWC's placement ultimately proved beneficial, as surrounding theaters and performances draw millions of visitors annually in the Cultural District. Within the 65,000 square foot center, visitors can explore exhibit galleries, a music cafe, education center, and a 486-seat theater.

The building's distinct architectural feature is the curvilinear form at the corner of the site, inspired from full sails of dhow (ships) in Swahili culture. The form also serves as an art piece and focal point of the surrounding intersection. AWC's namesake honors August Wilson, a world-renowned, local born playwright whose engagement and influence of Black culture transcended well beyond the city.

Despite being a permanent home for African American culture, AWC has faced backlash and hardship. While the center offers a contemporary appeal, its simplistic form, lack of material detail, and processional space have been harshly critiqued. Additionally, in 2013 AWC was forced into foreclosure after having operated in a deficit since its opening. Its closing, however, moved the city, leading to the Heinz Endowments, Richard King Mellon Foundation, and Pittsburgh Foundation, along with city support, coming together and purchasing the center the following year. Under new leadership, AWC has secured its financial future and once again serves the cultural scene of Pittsburgh's African American community.

Selected Accolades: Honor Award - AIA Pittsburgh (2010)

BEACON HILL RESIDENCES

DEVAN CASE and JONATHAN COLE *(Pendulum)*

Kansas City, MO (2016)

The Beacon Hill neighborhood has experienced numerous transformations since the early 1900s; however, none have been as significant as the recent gentrification of the community. Since the 2008 economic depression, numerous vacant lots have been bought and converted into high-priced homes, valued much higher than long-standing residences. Much of the Beacon Hill renaissance can be attributed to the Kietzman family, who relocated to the area in 2008. To the surprise of many people, their new home was located just steps from Troost Avenue, the unofficial color line between Blacks and Whites in Kansas City. The Kietzmans built a home worth $750,000, enticing many upper middle class residents to settle in the neighborhood.

The renaissance presented many commissioned projects for architects, including the local Black-owned firm Pendulum. Tasked with creating two contemporary homes targeted towards young professionals, the firm produced two houses with a similar approach to massing and materials; however, they are visually separated by contrasting roof conditions and color. On approach, visitors are greeted by a concrete box, encouraging residents to garden in a manageable space. Behind the planter is a wood-clad entry, creating a warm and inviting threshold between public and private space. Differing from traditional residences is the home's layout, as public areas (kitchen, dining, and living rooms) are located on the second floor, while bedrooms and additional private spaces reside on the lower level. This arrangement is also aided by the home's slope, as the residences are accessed through the second floor from garages located in a back alley.

While some residents perceived Beacon Hill's redevelopment as positive, many existing African American residents felt a growing tension between the 'haves' and 'have-nots'.[1] The neighborhood, once known as Millionaire's Row in the early 1900s, experienced a dramatic decline in businesses and residences as it underwent White Flight. Beacon Hill transformed into a predominantly Black community and maintained proud residents, even through the harsh realities of blight and crime. In the 1990s, the city revealed a plan to revitalize the neighborhood, largely due to its attractive views and proximity to downtown. Though the plan failed, the affluent middle class quickly purchased vacant lots and seemingly overnight transformed Beacon Hill into a diverse mix of residents. While many Black residents are thrilled over increased property values, others are equally afraid of being pushed out. The current Beacon Hill neighborhood stands as a break in the color line, but for how much longer remains to be seen.

[1] Adler, Eric, and Aaron Randle. 2017. (p.96)

BERKLEY SQUARE

PAUL WILLIAMS

Las Vegas, NV (1954)

By the end of World War II, the Black population in Las Vegas increased more than twenty-fold. Due to strict laws and customs, Blacks were regulated to the Westside and faced a housing shortage that put pressure on the city for more development. Additionally, recent changes in the Federal Housing Administration (FHA) regulations allowed Blacks to finance their own homes, creating a need for single-family residences to house the African American middle class.

Before the emergence of the African American middle class, 'Black' Las Vegas began in the early 1900s, when J.T. McWilliams purchased 88 acres of land. A few decades later, the government constructed a post office and courthouse, forcing the Black population to the west side of the city and the start of the West Las Vegas neighborhood. The neighborhood flourished with restaurants, club, and taverns, among many other Black-owned businesses. Many famous Black entertainers, including Sammy Davis Jr. and Lena Horne, stayed in hotels in West Las Vegas, as they were barred from accomodations hosting their performances due to Jim Crow laws.

In 1947, investors and the City of Las Vegas petitioned the FHA to develop "a new 2-bedroom project for colored people.[1]" Paul Williams, the most famous black architect in America at the time, was chosen early on to design a 40-acre development. Though several changes occurred by Berkley Square's opening in 1955 (including its name, as it formerly was named Westside Park), Williams' design remained constant, aided by his understanding of governmental planning regulations. The ranch-style homes were simple, sturdy, and allowed some flexibility in appearance. Their success was immediate, leading to waiting lists for new homes. In the 1960s and 70s, the city focused on desegregation, causing many Blacks to disperse from West Las Vegas. Though former residents have relocated to other parts of the city, Berkley Square remains a legacy to the aspirations of many African American families.

Selected Accolades: National Register of Historic Places (2009), Las Vegas Historical Designation (2014)

[1] "Berkley Square Historic District, Las Vegas, Nevada." (p.97)

BIRMINGHAM CIVIL RIGHTS INSTITUTE

J. MAX BOND JR. *(Bond, Ryder, James), John Brown and Associates*
Birmingham, AL (1992)

The Birmingham Civil Rights Institute (BCRI) stands near the aftermath of one of the most disturbing moments of the Civil Rights era. Directly across the street is the site of the 1963 bombing of Sixteenth Street Baptist Church, killing four African American girls. BCRI also faces Kelly Ingram Park, host to Black protesters who were hosed and attacked by police dogs the same year. With history encompassing the site and city, BCRI's placement appropriately entails the struggles of the Civil Rights movement.

The idea of a community 'march' personifies the entry into the institute. A pathway slopes upward, leading to an entry court, culminating with a central rotunda. While reminiscent of domed churches, the rotunda is not monumental in scale. The entire 58,000 square foot building utilizes brick and roof formations that fit neatly into the Birmingham landscape. Gestures to African and African American culture, through details and geometry, further suggest strong ties to the community. Additionally, BCRI acknowledges its surroundings by creating a wide public space set back from the park that aligns with Sixteenth Street Baptist Church. Inside, museum visitors are reminded harshly of past times. Provoking displays and unsettling memorabilia spark conversations about past, present, and future directions of civil rights. The museum's procession ends in a light-filled gallery, with framed views of the church and Kelly Ingram Park. It is the hope that within BCRI's walls, racial tensions will resolve and lead to better relations in the community and nation.

Though a museum was sorely lacking in the community, the residents of Birmingham were less than thrilled to rehash old wounds and increase taxes. Only through the persistence of the city's first Black mayor, Richard Arrington Jr. (1979-1999), was BCRI able to obtain the requisite funds to open its doors. Through his efforts, the museum has become a catalyst for change to its surroundings, including the larger contextual design of the Civil Rights District. The new community includes the Alabama Jazz Hall of Fame, Carver Theatre, and a historic neighborhood of Black businesses. In addition, BCRI's popularity and critical acclaim have cemented its place as one of the best and most influential civil rights museums in the United States.

Selected Accolades: Accreditation - American Alliance of Museums (2005), Affiliation - Smithsonian Institute (2007), Birmingham Civil Rights National Monument (2017)

BOOKER T. WASHINGTON RESIDENCE

ROBERT R. TAYLOR

Tuskegee, AL (1899)

The Oaks, home of Booker T. Washington, rests on the campus of Tuskegee University. Washington believed African Americans could obtain success and equality if given proper education. Through his ideology and efforts, the Tuskegee Normal and Industrial Institute opened in 1881. As the school's first president, until his death in 1915 Washington oversaw more than 100 buildings constructed within the campus that offered nearly 40 different trades.

Using bricks crafted by their own hands, Tuskegee's students constructed Washington's home. The residence was the first of its kind in the county to have electricity and running water. The 7,800 square foot Queen Anne style house was designed by the first Black MIT graduate, Robert R. Taylor, and solidified the notion that African Americans have craftsmanship equal to Whites. Interior period details crafted locally by students and tradesmen further proved this notion. Unique features include friezes depicting Washington's travels to Europe, walls covered in paint

invented by George Washington Carver, and a claw foot bathtub. Washington also owned a desk belonging to former president Abraham Lincoln.

The Oaks gained popularity through Washington's involvement in civil rights and educational outreach. During the 25th anniversary of the university in 1906, many prominent people visited the home, including William Howard Taft, Harvard president Charles W. Eliot, and Andrew Carnegie. The Oaks also hosted a reception for President Theodore Roosevelt. Washington remained in his home until his death in 1915, and his wife until her passing in 1925. In 1974, The Oaks was acquired by the National Park Service, becoming part of the Tuskegee Institute National Historic Site. Presently, the home accommodates 25,000 annual visitors and serves as a reminder of Booker T. Washington's legacy and the power of Black achievement.

Selected Accolades: Tuskegee Institute National Historic Site (1974)

CARNEGIE LIBRARY

MOSES MCKISSACK III *(McKissack & McKissack)*
Nashville, TN (1909)

Carnegie Library, located on the grounds of Fisk University, was designed by the architectural firm McKissack & McKissack, whose family has roots in the trade dating back to the early nineteenth century. The McKissack family's lineage traces back to Moses McKissack, a slave originating from the Ashanti tribe of West Africa. As a slave, Moses learned the craft of a master builder. The trade was then passed along to Moses McKissack III, who opened a practice in 1905 in Nashville. His first significant project was Carnegie Library, which catapulted his career into becoming one of the most prominent Black architects of his generation.

The Carnegie Library was made possible by a $20,000 contribution from philanthropist Andrew Carnegie. Matching funds from Fisk University and alumni were also secured, paving the way for a larger facility to hold an expanding collection. In 1908, ground was broken for the new building, with the cornerstone being laid a month later by future president William Howard Taft. The two-story, 10,125 square foot brick building was constructed in a restrained Neo-Classical style and contains a lightwell to illuminate interior spaces. Interior walls and furniture used polished oak, while floors were covered in cork to minimize noise. In addition to holding nearly 9,000 volumes, the Carnegie Library housed a women's gym, seminar rooms, and residences for female boarders. After its completion, the library was deemed one of the most elegant buildings in the south and considered one of the more prominent works by an African American architect in the nation.

By the mid-1920s, collection growth and changing demands of the university prompted Fisk to remodel Carnegie Library. Additional offices, classrooms, and collection space provided ample and aesthetic upgrades for the building. A year later, however, the university received a grant from the General Education Board, which prompted the construction of a brand new library. In 1930, Carnegie Library's collection was vacated, though the facility continues to be used as an academic building. Though its tenure as a library was brief, the legacy of the building lives on as a tribute to Moses McKissack III and Fisk University's early history.

Selected Accolades: Fisk University Historic District (1978), National Register of Historic Places (1985)

CHARLES H. WRIGHT MUSEUM OF AFRICAN AMERICAN HISTORY

HAROLD VARNER *(Sims Varner & Associates)*

Detroit, MI (1997)

The origin of the Charles H. Wright Museum dates back to 1965, when Dr. Charles Wright traveled to Denmark and experienced a memorial dedicated to service members of War World II. The trip inspired Wright to honor the African-American experience by preserving their history, life, and culture. In conjunction with several other advocates, the museum opened as the International Afro-American Museum. Its collection housed a wide variety of African American artifacts, including items from both African and American cultures. Success quickly followed, causing the museum to outgrow its building.

In 1978, the city of Detroit agreed to lease land to the museum. By 1987, the new facility opened, five times larger than the previous building, which also ushered in a name change to the Museum of African American History. At only 28,000 square feet, the museum once again outgrew its space and required a larger building. In 1992, Detroit voters authorized the sale of construction bonds to finance a third building. The newest facility officially opened its doors in 1997 as the Charles H. Wright Museum of African

American History, with 125,000 square feet of space. At the time, it was the largest African American historical museum in the world.

The museum contains more than 35,000 items, comprised of the Blanche Coggin Underground Railroad Collection, Harriet Tubman Museum Collection, and Coleman A. Young Collection. Additionally, the Wright Museum contains several large exhibits and features, most notably the Ford Freedom Rotunda (containing a dome nearly the same size as the U.S. Capitol), Ring of Genealogy, and Inspiring Minds: African Americans in Science and Technology S.T.E.M. exhibit. Collections range from local history to national movements to international cultures. The museum also accommodates large events, including a memorable viewing of a passed Rosa Parks in 2005, attended by tens of thousands of visitors. Through continued support from individuals and groups, the Charles H. Wright Museum of African American History remains an iconic landmark in Detroit, as well as across the world.

DUKE UNIVERSITY CAMPUS BUILDINGS

JULIAN ABELE *(Horace Trumbauer)*

Durham, NC (1925-1947)

It is a bit surprising that the architect responsible for the majority of Duke University's original buildings never stepped foot on campus. Julian Abele, the architect of Duke's new campus, never visited his numerous projects due to segregation. Despite his talent, many buildings were not signed by his hand until his firm's founder, Horace Trumbauer, passed away in 1938, and it would remain another 40 years until his contributions were properly acknowledged by the university.

The origins of Duke University are traced back to 1838, when Methodist and Quaker families employed a teacher for their subscription school in rural Randolph County. Waning Quaker support forced the school to seek state aid, leading to the founding of the Normal School in 1851. Slow progress in North Carolina's public school system led to a partnership with the Methodist Episcopal Church, creating a steady stream of financial support and a change of the school's name to Trinity College in 1859. A change in curriculum and philosophy prompted the college's relocation to Durham in 1892, in hopes of attracting more students in an urban setting. A $100,000 endowment helped sponsor the move, provided by the wealthy Methodist Washington Duke.

Though Trinity College prospered in its new environment, plans for a university campus materialized in the 1920s. Under the guidance of James B. Duke (the younger brother of Washington Duke), the Duke Endowment (a $40 million trust fund) established Duke University and the separate Woman's College on Trinity's grounds (the campuses merged in 1972). The team of Horace Trumbauer designed several buildings in the traditional Collegiate Gothic style (Duke) and Georgian manner (Woman's College). Duke's campus is centered around Duke Chapel, a 210-foot high, imposing structure characterized by its vast interior space and beautiful stonework. By the early 1930s, dozens of buildings were constructed, as the campuses were responsible for the largest Depression-era project in the United States.

While records of Julian Abele's work were accessible, it was not until the 1980s that students realized his contributions to Duke University. The 1986 protests of the campus' involvement in South Africa's apartheid system sparked mixed reactions and protests; however, Abele's granddaughter, a student at Duke, penned a letter stating the campus itself was a perfect example of "what a Black man can create given the opportunity.[1]" The letter likened apartheid to Jim Crow laws and discussed Duke's segregation of Blacks, which was lifted in 1961. Her reaction sparked a campus and nationwide movement to recognize Abele's contributions. Presently, Duke proudly hangs two of his portraits in prominent buildings, and in 2016 the Abele Quad was established, surrounded by original academic and residential buildings. Duke is also in the process of making Abele's role in the university's early history more prominent.

[1] Tifft, Susan E. 2015. (p.104)

DUSABLE MUSEUM OF AFRICAN AMERICAN HISTORY

WENDELL CAMPBELL *(Wendell Campbell Associates)*

Chicago, IL (expansion 1993)

The DuSable Museum of African American History, founded in 1961, remains the oldest museum continuously dedicated to the African American experience. With well over ten thousand historic items, the DuSable Museum is surpassed only by the National Museum of African American Heritage and Culture. Formerly known as the Ebony Museum of Negro History, the collection began in the home of Dr. Margaret Burroughs, a historian, writer, and teacher at DuSable High School. Similar to many museums founded during the Civil Rights era, the Ebony Museum arose from Black awareness. Inspiration from W.E.B. Dubois inspired Dr. Burroughs to preserve and display African American history and culture. Through her passion, a growing collection and community support led to a new location in 1968, as well as a name change to reflect Chicago's Black founder, Jean Baptiste DuSable.

Five years later, the DuSable Museum relocated to its current home, the former South Park Administration Building, in Washington Park. Esteemed architect Daniel Burnham designed the Beaux Arts facility in 1910, noted for its perfected poured concrete details and informal architectural manner, which was often designed in park structures. The museum's new location attracted funding from the parks district and private donors, allowing the building to increase its collection extensively and acquire objects from West Africa, artifacts from the Civil War and slavery, and photographs of the Great Migration. Items from prominent African Americans were also obtained, including the desks of W.E.B. Dubois and Chicago's first Black mayor, Harold Washington, the boxing gloves of Joe Louis, and the christening gown of Langston Hughes.

A 1993 expansion added a brutalist two-story wing, led by Wendell Campbell, the first president of the National Organization of Minority Architects (NOMA). The addition, named after Harold Washington, doubled the size of the museum by adding an auditorium, gallery spaces, research library, and an outdoor garden. In 2004, the DuSable Museum acquired the nearby vacant 61,000 square foot Roundhouse, an 1880 Burnham design, in hopes of forming the nation's first African American museum campus. Interior renovations proved difficult (an exterior restoration was completed in 2012), as an economic downturn and Barack Obama's presidential campaign siphoned funds away from the museum. A lack of leadership, low attendance, and few amenities also contributed to the Roundhouse's slow development. In recent years, a reduced vision promises to complete a renovation before the 2021 opening of the nearby Barack Obama Presidential Center.

FIRST AFRICAN METHODIST EPISCOPAL CHURCH

PAUL WILLIAMS

Los Angeles, CA (1968)

The First African Methodist Episcopal (FAME) Church was founded by Bridget 'Biddy' Mason, a slave who arrived with her owner in Los Angeles in 1856. California was a free state, allowing Mason to win her freedom with the help of local Black and White abolitionists. In 1872, the first meeting of FAME was organized in Mason's home, attended by twelve people. The congregation remained stagnant until migrations of African Americans in the 1880s significantly increased membership, resulting in the first permanent church opening its doors in 1903. The Gothic style building quickly became a landmark within the African American community.

Over the next 60 years, the neighborhood surrounding FAME transformed into industrial and commercial properties, prompting the church to find a new home in a residential setting. In addition, upgrades to services increased the church's presence in the community; however, space constraints became a significant issue contributing to the need for a larger building. Prominent African American architect Paul Williams supplied plans for a new worship space in the early 1960s, which included a 5,000 seat sanctuary, 150 seat chapel, and two auditoriums with capacities of 600 and 700 people, respectively. Fundraising for the new building crossed racial barriers as many Hollywood stars, including Marlon Brando and Danny Thomas, contributed donations and assisted in breaking ground. Following the church's completion, the congregation marched from their past home to the present, led by the pastor and prominent stars, many of whom were members of the church.

Williams designed the new FAME church in a late Modern architectural style (his funeral was held at the church in 1980). The 11,366 square foot building rests on an elevated foundation to exert its presence within the community. A zigzag motif utilized along the roof line and porch of the entrance contrasts with the simple stucco exteriors. The church also features murals in-between the bays of the western facade to relieve the monotonous walls. In addition to maintaining its current facility, FAME remains persistent in its social welfare. Each year, the church spends more than two million dollars to fund dozens of programs that help nurture youth, elderly, and homeless facilities throughout the Los Angeles community.

Selected Accolades: Fisk University Historic District (1978), National Register of Historic Places (1985)

FRANCIS GREGORY LIBRARY

DAVID ADJAYE *(Adjaye Associates), Wiencek Associates*
Washington D.C. (2012)

Francis Gregory Library (formally Friends of the Francis A. Gregory Regional Library) opened in 1961 as the fifth of eleven libraries funded through the D.C. Public Works Program. Designed by Victor W. DeMers, the building was located in the Fort Davis neighborhood, an African American community named for its former Civil War fort. The library opened as the Fort Davis branch and remained so named until 1986, when the community advocated for the building to reflect the name of the library's Board of Trustees' first Black president, Francis A. Gregory.

The need for a library arose in the early 1950s, after the development of Fort Davis in the 1940s. Plans for the branch were put on hold after the construction of the nearby Anacostia Library took precedence. In 1953, a site adjacent to wooded surroundings was selected; however, the land was considered federal property and required three years of negotiations for proper use. Construction began

in 1959 and was completed nearly six months past its scheduled completion due to a steelworkers' strike. With 18,000 square feet of space, Fort Davis library boasted traditional library amenities: an adult reference area and soundproof listening room on the first floor; children's space and staff areas on the second level; and a community room in the basement. The library, constructed of brick and concrete, was heralded as an excellent example of modern and functional architecture.

The library was designated a regional branch in 1977, increasing its collection, public access, and administration. Over time, the needs of the community outgrew the building, leading to a competition for a 21st-century replacement in the late 2000s. David Adjaye, the iconic British-Ghanaian architect, won the competition for a new Francis Gregory Library, as well as the local William O. Lockridge/Bellevue Library.

The new 22,500 square foot Francis Gregory Library lies in stark contrast with its former building. While the original library was a simple box, the new design aims to become a landmark and premier social gathering space of the Fort Davis and nearby communities. The light-filled building blends with its wooded surroundings through a mixture of transparent and diamond-patterned, reflective glass. Inside, the dynamic exterior gives way to a soft wood clad curtain wall. Warm wood is also used in flexible meeting spaces, which cantilever from the second level. The upper-level children's room uses the notion of a floating volume to create an intriguing space for its visitors, allowing glimpses of the woods in the likeness of a treehouse. With ample social spaces and vibrant areas for adults, children, and teens, the Francis Gregory Library has enjoyed a warm welcome from its community.

Selected Accolades: LEED Silver, Honor Award - AIA Maryland (2015)

Harvey B. Gantt Center
for African-American Arts+Culture

THE HEWITT
COLLECTION

HARVEY B. GANTT CENTER FOR AFRICAN AMERICAN ARTS & CULTURE

PHILIP FREELON *(The Freelon Group)*

Charlotte, NC (2009)

The Harvey B. Gantt Center for African American Arts & Culture commemorates the achievements of African Americans throughout American history. The building also serves as a community hub for music, dance, theater, visual art, film, arts education programs, literature, and outreach. Located in Charlotte's historic Brooklyn neighborhood, the Gantt Center resides in what was once a thriving Black community during the early 20th century.

The iconic skin of the 46,500 square foot building is inspired by the exterior stairs of the former Myers Street School, the only public school for Blacks in the late 1800s. Many students affectionately referred to the exterior stairs as 'Jacob's Ladder'. The stairs were not only a means of access, but a symbol of hope, pride, and advancement among African Americans. Jacob's Ladder continues in the Gantt Center through its stairs and escalators, which usher visitors to the second-floor lobby from both ends of the building.

Perforated exterior panels also use motifs from historical Black culture. The panels are 'stitched' together, reminiscent of African textiles and quilt designs from the Underground Railroad era. The arrangement forms a rain screen, interrupted only by windows where interior daylight is necessary. Panels on the center's backside are uninterrupted by windows due to future development. Accented strip lighting illuminates selected panel edges, stimulating an inspiring metaphor of achievement.

As a center of celebration and inspiration, the building's architecture thrives and compliments the institution's mission. The Gantt Center's message to present, preserve, and promote African American culture is realized through its design. With ample, flexible space to house collections from world-renowned artists and museums, a rooftop terrace, and visual appeal, the Gantt Center thrives as a beacon in the Charlotte and African American communities.

Selected Accolades: Honor Award - AIA North Carolina (2010)

HOWARD THEATRE

MICHAEL MARSHALL *(Marshall Moya Design), Martinez and Johnson Architecture*
Washington D.C. (renovation 2012)

The Howard Theatre opened its doors in 1910 to a predominantly African American community in Washington D.C. The theater was designed by J. Edward Storck and is named for its proximity to Howard University. As one of the early significant entertainment venues for African Americans, the Howard Theatre attracted many high profile musicians and entertainers. Duke Ellington, Ella Fitzgerald, Sammy Davis Jr., and Lena Horne were just a few of the performers to grace the theater's stage. With seating for 1,200, the venue also accommodated live theater, musicals, local talent shows, and theatrical companies. Balls and other receptions attracted famous actors and stars, including President Franklin Roosevelt and his wife, Eleanor.

In 1941, the theater underwent renovations that transformed its blend of Beaux-Arts, Neoclassical, and Italian Renaissance architecture to a contemporary Streamline style. More changes in the 1950s resulted in the loss of middle and upper class patronage as the theater became a venue for rhythm and blues artists, attracting teenage and young adult crowds. Desegregation and the 1968 riots caused a further decline in the Howard Theatre's attendance, which also led to an unsafe surrounding community. A revival attempt in 1975 was short-lived, as the venue hosted only sporadic events before closing and falling into disrepair for more than 30 years.

A successful revival prevailed through the Howard Theatre Restoration group's acquisition of capital to restore the building. Renovation of the 30,390 square foot building incorporated a tasteful mix of 21st century style with the original 1910 design. The modern aesthetic, designed by the team of Michael Moya, is defined by a full-service restaurant and kitchen, two Brazilian granite bars, custom signage, and additional sophisticated elements. Most significant is the addition of light boxes, illuminating important past performers of the Howard Theatre. The renovated venue is home to live performances, corporate meetings, and 'Sunday Gospel' brunches, creating a multi-functional facility for the community. With much of the original design preserved, the Howard Theatre has regained its iconic status within the Black community.

Selected Accolades: Excellence in Historic Resources - AIA Washington D.C. (2012), Renovation Honorable Mention - International Design Awards (2013), Presidential Citation - AIA (2013)

IBERVILLE HOUSING PROJECTS

WM. RAYMOND MANNING *(Manning Architects)*, *Concordia, HCI Architecture*
New Orleans, LA (2015-2019)

The Iberville Housing Projects opened in 1941 under the newly formed Housing Authority of New Orleans (HANO). Seventy-five residences replaced Storyville, the former red light district of the city, which began in 1897 under councilman Sidney Story's ordinance, confining prostitution to an area adjacent to downtown. Jazz clubs and brothels thrived at the turn of the century; however, interest in prostitution waned over time, as by 1915 more than one-half of all brothels were vacated. In 1917, the U.S. Department of Navy forced the closure of Storyville, abruptly ending the city's experiment. Over the next twenty years, the district's slum remains were removed, paving the way for HANO's first housing project.

Iberville, as well as other affordable housing projects in the 1940s, was spurred by the Great Depression. Rampant homelessness led to the United States Housing Act of 1937 (the Wagner Bill), allowing federal funds to aid in the construction of low-income housing. New Orleans was the first city in the U.S. to benefit from the act, and Iberville was the third of six local affordable housing projects funded through the approved bill. Under HANO's guidance, architects Hubert A. Benson, George H. Christy, and William Spink designed 858 apartments that recall 19th-century rowhouses. The Georgian brick buildings blend in scale and aesthetic with surrounding neighborhoods, characterized by gabled ends, chimneys, and elaborate ironwork.

Iberville initially accommodated White servicemen and the working class, but over time its demographic shifted to low-income African American families. The migration of industries away from the city and 'White flight' in the 1960s plunged the complex into poverty. Officials took note of the blighted community and coveted its redevelopment for its proximity to the French Quarter and downtown neighborhoods. Plans for a sports stadium, music museum, and big-box retailer were proposed in the early 2000s; however, much to the delight of Iberville residents, the plans failed to gain traction. In 2005, Hurricane Katrina ravaged New Orleans' infrastructure, paving the way for the city to redevelop Iberville. With displaced residents, many officials considered the hurricane to be the catalyst in the removal of the housing projects. This belief was expressed through Representative Richard Baker's controversial remark, "We finally cleaned up public housing in New Orleans. We couldn't do it. But God did.[1]"

Plans for a mixed-use development materialized, with the majority of Iberville's original residences marked for removal (sixteen are planned for preservation). The new community, renamed Bienville Basin, contains 700 market rate apartments and space for community and leisure activities. The 23-acre site is part of the larger Iberville/Tremé neighborhood redevelopment, comprised of 2,500 apartments, commercial, and recreational uses. With the project nearing completion, hundreds of low-income residences have been displaced, sparking fears of gentrification. Amid disasters of past local African American housing redevelopments, Iberville plans affordable one-to-one replacements within its neighborhood to accommodate past and low-income residents.

[1] Saulny, Susan. 2006. (p.103)

JOHN D. O'BRYANT
AFRICAN AMERICAN INSTITUTE

DONALD STULL and DAVID LEE *(Stull and Lee), William Rawn Associates*

Boston, MA (2006)

The roots of the John D. O'Bryant African American Institute date back to the late 1960s. Black students at Northeastern University in Boston lacked social and cultural activities on campus, although graduating was a primary focus. In 1968, the Civil Rights movement prompted Stokely Carmichael to speak at the university, and he urged students to form a chapter of the Student Non-Violent Coordinating Committee (SNCC). Carmichael's influence and the voices of other local organizations led to the formation of the Afro American Association (AAA). Following the assassination of Martin Luther King Jr., the AAA presented 13 demands to the president of Northeastern University, the last of which called for the creation of a committee to track the progress of their request. This demand was approved in 1969 by the president and board, thus forming the African American Institute.

Throughout the 1970s and 80s, the Institute successfully promoted cultural awareness of the African American community by implementing courses, social events, tutoring, a student newspaper, and recognition of achievement geared towards a Black audience. The organization's success gained the attention of the nation, attracting such prominent Black leaders as Jesse Jackson and Julian Bond. Additionally, the Institute increased its impact in the community through the efforts of John D. O'Bryant, vice president of Student Affairs, when the organization merged within the division. O'Bryant's passing in 1992 prompted the university to rename the Institute in his honor, commemorating his tireless efforts in advocacy and education.

The current home of the John D. O'Bryant African American Institute opened in 2006, located within the West Village F building, and contains an academic center, honors program, and housing. With 15,000 square feet of space, the Institute features state of the art facilities that include classrooms, exhibition space, computers, and a library of rare books and documents. A dramatic two-story facade inspired by African precedents honors the center's African American culture. In 2015, a portion of the Institute was renovated to create flexible space for students, catering to individuals, small groups, events, and other collaborations. Although many changes have occurred throughout its storied history, the John D. O'Bryant African American Institute continues to serve as a hub of academic, cultural, and social life among Black students at Northeastern University and the greater Boston community.

JOHNSON PUBLISHING BUILDING

JOHN WARREN MOUTOUSSAMY *(Dubin Dubin Black & Moutoussamy)*
Chicago, IL (1972)

The Johnson Publishing Building is the first and only high-rise designed by an African American architect in downtown Chicago. Once home to Jet and Ebony magazines, the building appears as a bland, conservative Modern structure overlooking Grant Park. The interior, however, was designed in a stylish contemporary manner, full of 1970s flair. Flower-like patterns and rectangular shapes line the walls, covered in gold and brown colors. Much of the interior furnishings and fixtures remain intact, a tribute to John Warren Moutoussamy's grid-like design of the building (heavily influenced by Mies van der Rohe).

The Chicago headquarters of Jet and Ebony is an achievement of John H. Johnson, the founder of both publications. The Johnson Publishing Company was established in 1942, with the launching of the Negro Digest. Three years later, Ebony magazine was introduced, with its first issue selling 50,000 copies. The general interest magazine made Johnson the owner of the nation's most widely circulated Black publication and the founder of the Black consumer market. Ebony's success led to the release of Jet, a weekly digest magazine introduced in 1951. With a net worth of $100 million by the 1980s, Johnson's accomplishments made him one of the country's most successful Black businessmen.

The success of the Johnson Publishing Company led to the opening of its much-anticipated headquarters. The new building opened to much fanfare in 1972, as one thousand people attended the ceremony. Several notable African Americans attended, including Reverend Jesse Jackson, Lena Horne, Shirley Chisholm, and Dick Gregory. John Lennon, Yoko Ono, and Chicago Mayor Richard Daley also participated in the celebration. Overwhelming support helped the Johnson Publishing Company remain in its building until 2010, when it moved its headquarters to the Borg-Warner Building. The building has remained vacant; however, plans from its new owners aim to convert the office space into 150 apartment units, while preserving exterior remnants of the original design.

Selected Accolades: Chicago Landmark (2017)

LANGSTON TERRACE DWELLINGS

HILYARD ROBINSON

Washington D.C. (1938)

Langston Terrace Dwellings opened as the second government-funded housing project in the United States, the first in the nation's capital. Construction began in 1935 as part of the New Deal initiative under President Franklin Roosevelt. The new program introduced a series of experimental government-backed projects designed to supply jobs and stability following the Great Depression. Langston Terrace sought to relieve working class and lower income African Americans by providing affordable living during a shortage of housing.

Hilyard Robinson's design of Langston Terrace aimed to provide dignified living conditions while uplifting the Black community. Architectural studies in Europe influenced his work, in particular the Bauhaus and Dutch Modernist movements and their ideas on public housing. Robinson planned for the fourteen-building complex to contain extensive indoor and outdoor living spaces, gardens, and playful concrete animals for children. Financial constraints reduced his vision; however, Robinson managed to infuse creativity by using cost-saving pre-cast concrete panels during construction, a process replicated in future projects across the country. In addition to its unique design, the 13-acre Langston Terrace complex was awarded a commission from the Treasury Art Program, resulting in Dan Olney's frieze, "The Progress of the Negro Race." The sculpture depicts African Americans involved in agriculture, industry, education, and the Great Migration. For the 274 families that succeeded in competing for residency, the housing project provided hope within a battered economy.

Langston Terrace remains architecturally significant not only as a forerunner in federal housing, but also as a tribute to John Mercer Langston, one of the most significant Black figures of his time. Langston served as an abolitionist and the nation's first elected African American congressman in 1890. His legacy of Black advancement and inspiration well-suited the purpose of Langston Terrace, further empowering African Americans in their pursuit of happiness. Poverty remains at the forefront of the complex; however, hope and inspiration through its architecture uplift its residents towards a better future.

Selected Accolades: National Register of Historic Places (1987)

MAKE IT RIGHT HOMES

GERALD BILLES *(Billes Partners)*, DAVID ADJAYE *(Adjaye Associates)*
New Orleans, LA (2008)

Hurricane Katrina ravaged much of New Orleans' Lower Ninth Ward, creating the need for sustainable and affordable housing. In 2007, two years after Hurricane Katrina, actor Brad Pitt visited the community and was shocked by the lack of progress. Pitt wanted to improve the Lower Ninth Ward by providing housing for displaced residents. In an act of generosity, the actor established the Make It Right Foundation, aimed at restoring the devastated neighborhood through the construction of 150 new homes.

The Make It Right Foundation garnered local, national, and international architects. Such 'starchitects' included David Adjaye (Asem-Pa House), Shigeru Ban, and Frank Gehry, all winners of the esteemed Pritzker Architecture prize. Each architect was responsible for designing homes using Cradle to Cradle design principals, or homes that use safe and renewable materials, energy, maintain high water quality, and honor social fairness and dignity. To date, more than one hundred homes have been constructed; however,

many starchitects have designed only one prototype, mainly due to budget constraints. With over 4,000 homes lost in the devastation, many leaders criticized Brad Pitt and his foundation's lavish spending on high quality architects and ill-fitting designs. Ironically, the most popular homes have been built by the local New Orleans firm of Billes Partners, who honed in on community desires and history.

Billes' homes are designed in contemporary shotgun and camelback layouts, a tribute to the community's architectural heritage. The homes vary from 1,000-2,000 square feet in size, are appropriated to family needs, and contain measures to counter flooding. Shotgun homes consist of a single story, with three to five rooms aligned in a row and no hall connection. Camelback designs increase the living space of shotgun construction by the addition of a second story in the rear, generally unaltering the front side of the residences. Most early shotgun residences had no side windows, as they were often built tightly near other homes. Their

origins in the United States trace back to the early 19th century, when Haitian refugees escaped to New Orleans and brought their native architecture. Originally, shotgun homes were associated with lower and middle classes; however, over time they became synonymous with the struggles of poor African Americans. Though often found in lower class neighborhoods, these homes help form tight-knit communities, specifically by their inclusion of porches.

In recent years, a significant number of Make It Right homes have experienced structural issues. Moldy wood and roof leakage have been primary concerns, leaving a few homes in disrepair and uninhabitable. Poor construction has not deterred most residents, as the foundation has agreed to repair damage and restore homes to their original beauty. Overall, Billes' designs and other Make It Right residences have proven to be a strong catalyst in the Lower Ninth Ward, as restorative efforts have assisted residents in returning to a once familiar, vibrant community.

MARTIN LUTHER KING JR. NATIONAL MEMORIAL

DERYL MCKISSACK *(McKissack and McKissack)*, PAUL S. DEVROUAX and MARSHALL PURNELL *(Devrouax & Purnell)*, ED JACKSON JR., *ROMA Design Group*

Washington D.C. (2011)

The Martin Luther King Jr. (MLK) National Memorial rests on a small four-acre plot along the shores of the Tidal Basin; however, its impact stretches far beyond its borders. In alignment with the Lincoln and Jefferson Memorials, the MLK Memorial completes a "visual line of leadership.[1]" It's also the first memorial to honor an African American on the National Mall, solidifying King's legacy in American history.

Though King suffered an untimely death in 1968, the idea of a memorial didn't gain traction until the 1980s, when members of King's fraternity, Alpha Phi Alpha, presented the idea to its directors. In 1996, the Senate and House of Representatives jointly passed a resolution authorizing the design of a memorial. Two years later, President Bill Clinton signed the motion, leading to the founding of the Memorial Foundation. By the year 2000, nearly one thousand entries competed for the memorial. The winning design was completed by the ROMA Design Group, with Devrouax + Purnell partnering for local expertise. Devrouax + Purnell fell out of favor with the Memorial Foundation, and in 2007 they were replaced with McKissack and McKissack, the largest Black owned architecture firm in the United States. The memorial was officially dedicated in

October 2011 by President Barack Obama, continuing the legacy and progress of King's life's work.

The MLK Memorial's design centers on natural elements that evoke an emotional response, inspired by King's "I Have A Dream" speech. Upon entering the site, visitors are gently guided to the Mountain of Despair. The two sides of the sculpture are separated by a narrow 12-foot wide path, symbolically representing a journey of struggle. After passing through the Mountain of Despair, visitors encounter the 30-foot Stone of Hope, an enormous sculpture seemingly overcome from the mountain. Overlooking the Tidal Basin is King himself, inscribed in the Stone of Hope, carved by Chinese sculptor Lei Yixin. Though Yixin received heavy criticism (related to race and his questionable past body of work), his work is undeniably remarkable. King's solemn position connotes his wait for progress and equality in American society. Further portraying his legacy is a 450-foot wall surrounding the sculptures, etched with fourteen quotations carefully selected by the Memorial Foundation. The quotes were chosen to remain relevant to future generations, as well as a living memorial to King's life.

[1] "About the Memorial." (p.96)

NATIONAL CENTER FOR CIVIL AND HUMAN RIGHTS

PHILIP FREELON *(The Freelon Group), HOK*

Atlanta, GA (2014)

While many civil rights museums strive to encompass the entirety of the subject, the National Center for Civil and Human Rights focuses on "the understanding and exploration of the individual's role in civil and human rights.[1]" The Center aims to inspire by providing individual accounts of others who have directly experienced such movements. This embodiment requires an intimate, thought-provoking setting, evident in the building's spaces and vision of empowerment.

The Center was first conceived in 2007 by Civil Rights leader Evelyn Lowery and former United Nations Ambassador Andrew Young. With aid from former Atlanta mayor Shirley Franklin, their efforts were overwhelmingly supported by corporations and the community. Through tireless efforts, The Center has become one of the few world institutions that bridge the American Civil Rights Movement with contemporary global struggles for human rights.

The design of the 42,500 square foot building is inspired by iconic global spaces that have experienced historic civil and human rights events: the National Mall in Washington D.C.; Tiananmen Square in Beijing; and Tahrir Square in Cairo. The Freelon/HOK team, winners of the Center's 2008 design challenge, describe the design as "inspired by the links that connect and empower individuals and groups of seemingly divergent interests to find common ground.[2]" Utilizing the steep slope of the site, the building connects two public plazas by a grand outdoor staircase. The lower level entrance opens onto a plaza containing a tasteful steel and glass water sculpture celebrating civil and human rights. The upper level plaza, some 30 feet in elevation change, faces the pedestrian plaza of Pemberton Place, which connects to the landmarks of Coca-Cola and the Georgia Aquarium.

The Center is composed of two curved walls, defining a "space for action[2]" for the building's various program. The walls resemble a hut and are clad in metal panels gesturing African woven fabric. Visitors enter through the Pemberton Place level (the middle level of the building) and are welcomed into an expansive lobby. From the lobby, visitors can explore The Center's interactive exhibits, Martin Luther King Jr. papers, and additional displays on the lower and upper levels. The sloping walls are most vivid in the third floor gallery, where the leaning mass adds gravity to the difficult yet powerful stories of civil and human rights. By experiencing The Center's architecture and exhibits, visitors leave with a sense of inspiration to continue and support equal rights for all.

Selected Accolades: LEED Gold, Honor Award - AIA Georgia (2015), Merit Award - AIA North Carolina (2015)

[1] Gerfen, Katie. 2015. (p.99); [2] "National Center for Civil and Human Rights / HOK + The Freelon Group". 2015. (p.101)

NATIONAL MUSEUM OF AFRICAN AMERICAN HERITAGE AND CULTURE

PHILIP FREELON, DAVID ADJAYE, J. MAX BOND JR. *(Freelon Adjaye Bond/Smith Group)*,
DERYL MCKISSACK *(McKissack & McKissack)*

Washington D.C. (2016)

The National Museum of African American Heritage and Culture (NMAAHC) celebrates the history and achievement of Blacks at a level unprecedented in history. Nearly a century in the making, the idea of a museum resulted in dozens of committees, meetings, and studies addressing the need for such a place. Racial divide and tension prevented the earlier construction of a NMAAHC. It was not until the 1990s that serious conversation and organization materialized, leading to President George W. Bush signing the NMAAHC action plan in 2001, and ultimately a site selection in 2006.

In 2008, six architecture teams were selected to design the museum. The winning proposal was submitted by a powerhouse of Black architects, Philip Freelon, David Adjaye, and J. Max Bond Jr. (FAB/S). NMAAHC's architectural design followed a classical order in its use of a base, shaft, and corona. The three-tiered corona takes its inspiration from wooden caryatids, an object found in Yoruban art in West Africa. The corona also reflects its surroundings, as the seven-degree angle matches that of the Washington Monument (another African and classical inspired design). Wrapping the corona are iron panels, reminiscent of African American iron craftsmen in southern states. The

panels are not solely decorative; the iron grills exhibit different opacities to provide optimum comfort during hot summer months.

Upon entering the 409,000 square foot NMAAHC, visitors pass underneath a welcoming green roof porch, recalling architectural roots from Africa and the African diaspora. Porches are often a social transition space, a link between the street and private life. The FAB/S team used this notion to create a gathering point for visitors that welcomes, protects, and prepares them for the harsh realities within the museum. In addition to the outstanding exterior procession, visitors are greeted by a large, open concourse, followed by experiences stemming from 'nested boxes.'[1] Form follows functions, embracing a sense of the American story told through an African American lens, as visitors delve deep into Black history and culture.

The NMAAHC serves as a symbol of remembrance, progress, and hope of African American culture. Its design fosters conversations of history and relations, with a mission of reconciliation, resilience, and equality towards a better America.

[1] Wilson, Mabel O. 2016. (p.105)

THE NEGRO BUILDING

WILLIAM SIDNEY PITTMAN

Norfolk, VA (1907)

The culmination of the famed National Museum of African American History and Culture (NMAAHC) is the result of more than 100 years of discussions and calls to action. The NMAAHC was also built on the backs of previous museums that attempted to permanently display African American achievement on a large scale. One such museum was the Negro Building, erected for the Jamestown Tercentennial Exposition. Under the direction of Giles B. Jackson, the Negro Building was a testament to Black achievement less than 50 years after the Civil War.

In 1901, the state of Virginia approved plans to celebrate the 300th anniversary of the Jamestown settlement. While previous expositions displayed Black progress, there were no initial plans for the tercentennial event. African American leaders disapproved of the state's decision and fought to exhibit at the exposition. Led by Jackson, a display of Black achievement was secured along with the necessary funding from donors and Congress. Though many critics, including Jackson's mentor Booker T. Washington, believed the building would function as a reminder of a Jim Crow society, approval from President Roosevelt assured critics that the display would serve as a "creditable exhibit of the achievements of [the African American] race.[1]"

The 60,000 square foot Negro Building contained many exhibitions that were categorized into educational, agricultural, business enterprises, inventions, literary, and artistic achievements, totaling approximately 3,000 exhibitors. The building itself was designed in a dignified classical manner, relaying the importance of its contents. Furthering the notion of Black achievement was Jackson's commitment to a cast of Black workers, as African Americans worked as laborers, contractors, suppliers, and financiers.

The Negro Building's exhibits were an inspiring accomplishment; however, they were not well-attended by Blacks or other fair visitors. Overall, the Jamestown Tercentennial Exposition failed to achieve half of its anticipated attendance, resulting in bankruptcy and a declaration by the New York Times as "the most colossal failure in the history of exhibitions.[1]" For its part, the Negro Building drew 3,000-12,000 visitors per day, although Jackson estimated only one percent of the African American population traveled to the exposition. An attempt was made to relocate displays to Richmond permanently, but the idea was met with severe political backlash. Ten years later, the site developed into a naval base, with many buildings removed for new accommodations, including the Negro Building. Its attempt as a large-scale museum of color proved unsuccessful; however, the exposition served as a forerunner in Black achievement and the foundation to the NMAAHC.

[1] Hintz, Eric S. 2016. (p.99)

PAUL L. DUNBAR HIGH SCHOOL

CURTIS J. MOODY *(Moody Nolan), EEK Architect*
Washington D.C. (2013)

Paul L. Dunbar High School was founded in 1870 as the Preparatory High School for Colored Youth. Its first class consisted of one teacher and 15 students, many of whom later taught at the school. As the first public high school for African Americans in the country, the program aimed to prepare students for college and university enrollment. The rigorous courses produced a high college admission rate, allowing many students acceptance into top universities such as Howard, Harvard, and Dartmouth universities. Success of the program was further proven during an 1899 test of Washington D.C.'s four public high schools, as M Street School (its name from 1891-1916) scored higher marks than two of the three White high schools.

In 1916, M Street School was renamed in honor of the late African American poet Paul L. Dunbar. The school continued to have a high academic threshold; however, many challenges began to arise. Lack of funding contributed to ongoing teacher shortages, lack of classroom space, and poor maintenance. Despite these challenges, Dunbar High School continued its success until the mid-1950s, when the landmark case Brown v. Board of Education drastically changed D.C.'s educational landscape. The case's desegregation verdict caused D.C. public schools to become products of their neighborhoods, transforming the magnet Dunbar High School to a poor performing institution in a low-income African American community.

Decreasing academic rates have not deterred Dunbar High School's journey to regain its former success. In 2013, a new facility opened its doors, replacing the fortress-like structure from 1977. The new 260,000 square foot building aims to increase public engagement and provide a better atmosphere conducive to academic success. Various views and vistas offer a sense of community, connecting the school to an adjacent park and neighboring context. The new facility draws connections from a 1917 predecessor's main space, as it's arranged into four academies that are organized by a broader public space known as 'the Armory.' Each of the four programs opens onto the Armory and circulation, forming a multipurpose area often used for school dances, fundraising events, and community forums. The new Dunbar High School provides civic pride in a challenging neighborhood and hopes to positively enhance the relationships of its students and community.

Selected Accolades: LEED Platinum, Grand Prize - Learning By Design (2013), Presidential Citation in Sustainable Design - AIA Washington D.C. (2014), Design Citation - NOMA (2016)

PHILIPS HOUSE

JOHN S. CHASE
Austin, TX (1964)

The house commissioned by Della Phillips is quite different from neighboring homes, as its mid-century Modern design starkly contrasts surrounding bungalows and ranches. Phillips, a prominent African American businesswoman and wife of the University of Texas' (UT) first African American graduate, gave John S. Chase full control over the house's design. The home combines aspects of commercial and residential design, such as the folded roof planes (demonstrated in Chase's other commissions) and travertine columns. Phillips' one desire was space for entertaining, which along with influence from Frank Lloyd Wright was the primary inspiration for the residence.

The 2,865 square foot Phillips residence rests in a hillside, accessed through a two-way garage and elevator that ascends to the main living space. The raised main level provides privacy from the road while allowing natural light to penetrate from all sides of the home. Interior wood finishes create a light and spacious atmosphere, yet dignify the residence. Presently, few updates have taken place, maintaining the original style sought by Chase's mid-century Modern design.

While John Chase designed many buildings in the Austin and Texas area, his journey to prominence was hard fought. Chase enrolled as the first African American at UT's School of Architecture two days after the Supreme Court ruled in favor of the desegregation of graduate schools (1950). His studies were met with racial grief, as he received hate mail and unfavorable undertones; however, he also received support from White peers and faculty. In 1952, Chase became UT's second African American graduate and was widely celebrated across UT's community. Though highly regarded for his skill set, Chase faced discrimination in finding a job, leading him to found his own firm. Through hard work and determination, he forged a successful career, including co-founding the National Organization of Minority Architects (NOMA) in 1971. Wright's prairie style influence largely defined Chase's work, including the Philips House, which continues to inspire generations of architects.

PYTHIAN TEMPLE

LOUIS BELLINGER
MILTON OGOT

Pittsburgh, PA (1928 & restoration 2010)

Africans Americans were often barred from attending White social venues, with only a select few having the honor of performing. In Pittsburgh, a need for a Black social center arose in the 1920s to provide entertainment for the community. The Black Knights of Pythias, a local chapter of fraternal African American construction workers, spearheaded an entertainment center in the city's Black Hill District and chose Louis Bellinger to design a new prominent building. Bellinger was one of approximately sixty African American architects in practice, compared to 22,000 White architects across the United States.

The four-story Pythian Temple contained an eclectic mix of English Tudor style and Art Deco trimmings. To provide a sense of Black ownership, the fraternity's coat of arms was positioned below the building's crenellations. Inside, a 5,000 square foot banquet and drill hall covered the first floor, while a mixed-use 6,000 square foot auditorium stood on the second level. The auditorium's flexible design accommodated concerts, performances, and basketball games. Upper floors housed offices and meeting rooms for the Black Knights of Pythias. Upon its completion, several days of parades welcomed the center, highlighted by 10,000 people attending the cornerstone dedication.

The Pythian Temple flourished and quickly became the most important entertainment venue for African Americans within the Pittsburgh region. Jazz concerts, battles of music, and orchestras performed by well known Black entertainers offered many visitors the chance to socialize. The building's largest event accommodated Duke Ellington's coronation as the 'King of Jazz' in 1932, attended by 3,000 people from across the nation. In 1935, Bob Ellis took over management of the Pythian Temple, outfitting the building with a skating rink and lavish ballroom, renamed "The Gold and Silver Ballroom." The renovated theater's most notable concert benefited the victims of a local flood, headlined by Louis Armstrong.

Financial problems and new management led the Pythian Temple to be renamed the New Grenada Theater in 1937. An updated Modern exterior, theater, and the Hill City Auditorium attracted top Black jazz musicians from around the country. In 1945, the famous Savoy Ballroom relocated to the theater, continuing to attract the likes of James Brown, Ike and Tina Turner, and the O'Jays. New Grenada Theater's success lasted through the 1960s, until the Civic Arena (primarily used for professional hockey matches) displaced thousands of Hill District residents. The theater closed in 1965, and one of the last performances took place there in the early 1970s. After nearly a thirty-year period of vacancy and deterioration, the theater secured funds from the Heinz Endowments and other organizations for an extensive restoration. The revived New Grenada Theater aims to become a catalyst within New Granada Square, a mixed-use development of retail, residences, and entertainment.

SAMUEL E. KELLY ETHNIC CULTURAL CENTER

BENJAMIN F. MCADOO JR.
SAM CAMERON *(Rolluda Architects)*

Seattle, WA (1972 & 2013)

University of Washington's (UW) Samuel E. Kelly Ethnic Cultural Center opened as one of the first centers of its kind on a college campus. Similar to many other universities in the 1960s, UW experienced parallel protests to national movements, including civil rights, diversity, and opposition to the Vietnam War. In 1970, Samuel E. Kelly, an African American vet and doctoral graduate, was appointed as vice president of Minority Affairs, an organization geared towards the needs and success of minority students. During the same year, a new building was approved, and two years later it opened as the Ethnic Cultural Center. When completed, the center was the first building of its kind that housed a multitude of minority organizations in a single facility. Under Kelly's guidance, the center flourished and has helped thousands of minority students navigate their college careers.

The Ethnic Cultural Center, confined to a one-story building, contained 8,000 square feet. The building was organized around a central interior courtyard, flanked by offices and a library to the west and additional offices and conference space to the east. Classrooms and recreation space supplied ample support for the center's four core ethnic groups – African Americans, Hispanics, Asians, and Native Americans – providing students the opportunity to study their culture and history. Over the next few decades, the center remained largely unaltered in appearance. In 2001, decks on the north and south facades were enclosed, as well as the courtyard. The enclosure of the courtyard allowed protection from elements and increased interior space.

During the 2000s, the center outgrew its space as it boasted more than 60 student groups. Under the guidance of Rolluda Architects, a new three-story building replaced it, creating a welcoming environment for students of all backgrounds. The 26,000 square foot center, renamed in honor of Kelly, contains a large atrium and gathering space surrounded by public and private rooms for students and staff. A focus on natural light and sustainability (e.g., the wood clad exterior) provide an attractive and contemporary space. The building was designed by former UW students, including Sam Cameroon ('75), and contains 22 murals from the original building. The Samuel E. Kelly Ethnic Cultural Center continues to serve a diverse student population and stands as the oldest and largest cultural center in the U.S.

Selected Accolades: LEED Gold

SCHOMBURG CENTER FOR RESEARCH IN BLACK CULTURE

J. MAX BOND JR. *(Bond, Ryder, and Associates)*
New York City, NY (1980)

The Schomburg Center for Research in Black Culture is an international leader of collections highlighting the African American experience. The center's origins date back to 1905, as the Division of Negro Literature, History and Prints located in Harlem. One year later, the Division gained international recognition through the addition of Arturo Alfonso Schomburg's personal collection. His collection contained more than 10,000 books, manuscripts, etchings, paintings, and pamphlets. In 1940, the Division changed its name to the Schomburg Collection of Negro Literature, History and Prints, and in 1972 to its current name.

1972 also marked the Schomburg's designation as a research institution for the New York Public Library. The new designation prompted a need for a new building to house expanding collections. Designed by J. Max Bond Jr., the Schomburg Center draws inspiration from African aesthetics, influenced by his time visiting Africa. The octagonal design of the reading rooms stems from African influences of churches constructed by slaves. Within the first level gallery, glimpses of the outside world promote a sense of community and connection in the building.

By the late 1980s, the Schomburg Center's essential need in Harlem propelled the city to renovate and add a theater, gift shop, exhibition hall, and collection space. Presently, the center houses over ten million items and continues to thrive as a cultural institution in the Black community. In recent years The Center has experienced extensive renovations, including increased interior public space and digital signage over the lobby. Despite these improvements, the spirit of the 1980 building remains intact and continues to inspire excellence in Black culture and achievement.

SIXTEENTH STREET BAPTIST CHURCH

WALLACE RAYFIELD

Birmingham, AL (1911)

Sixteenth Street Baptist Church is one of the most prominent buildings of the Civil Rights movement. Founded in 1871, the church was the first Black congregation in the city of Birmingham, and was originally known as the First Colored Baptist Church of Birmingham. During the mid-1880s, the congregation erected a Gothic Revival building on the present day site; however, structural issues forced its deconstruction. The church turned to one of the nation's few professional Black architects, Wallace Rayfield, for a more stable structure. The replacement building is composed of varied brown colored brick that rests on a dark brown sandstone plinth. Bell towers with arched pyramidal roofs flank the main facade, forming a symmetrical design. An additional dome rises from the center of the building, marking the intersection of the transepts and the nave.

During the 1950s and 60s, the Sixteenth Street Baptist Church became synonymous with the struggle for civil rights. Birmingham was notorious for White supremacy, causing many activists to focus their efforts on desegregating the city and surrounding South. Many protest marches began on the steps of the church, as the building served not only as a leading place of worship, but as a gathering place for civil rights activities. Its spacious building and proximity to the historic Kelly Ingram Park also played a role in its spotlight. Such activities included meetings by the Alabama Christian Movement for Human Rights (ACMHR), which was established in 1956 by the Reverend Fred Shuttlesworth and assumed social efforts after the NAACP was barred from Alabama. Resultant actions by the ACMHR in lawsuits, boycotts, and nonviolent actions did little to ease racial tensions in the city.

Early in 1963, Shuttlesworth reached out to Martin Luther King Jr. to plan a series of nonviolent campaigns. The Sixteenth Street Baptist Church became the start of daily protest marches that saw hundreds arrested and jailed. Many of these events were met with severe police brutality, and images of fire hoses and dogs attacking civil rights activists shocked the nation. On a Sunday morning in September 1963, members of the Ku Klux Klan detonated a bomb in the church, injuring more than 20 people and killing four young girls: Addie Mae Collins, Cynthia Wesley, Carole Robertson, and Denise McNair. The attack was the direct result of a federal court order mandating the integration of Alabama's school system.

Following the bombing, a wave of outrage and support encased the city. Thousands of Black protesters gathered at the scene, triggering a wave of violence among protesters, police, and the National Guard. The protesting efforts proved useful, as they led to the passing of the Civil Rights Act of 1964 and Voting Rights Act of 1965. As for the church, restoration efforts quickly took place, and by June 1965 services resumed. Support reached international levels, including a stained glass representation of a Black Christ donated by the citizens of Wales. In recent decades, the Sixteenth Street Baptist Church, Kelly Ingram Park, and its surroundings have evolved to offer a complete context of civil rights activities within Birmingham.

SOJOURNER FAMILY PEACE CENTER

ISAAC MENYOLI *(M&E Architects), Zimmerman Architectural Studios*
Milwaukee, WI (2015)

The Sojourner Family Peace Center aims to reduce domestic violence in the greater Milwaukee area. The 72,000 square foot complex, a consolidation of three facilities, provides multiple services for victims of domestic violence and their families, through affordable and integrated services. Services include crisis housing, system advocacy, and individual support. The center also has partnerships with the Children's Hospital of Wisconsin, Milwaukee Police Department, child protective services, and health agencies. The Sojourner Family Peace Center serves as the largest child and family violence advocacy center in the country and stands as a strong presence within the community.

The treatment of victims is the driving force behind the center's design. Of significant concern is privacy, an approach taken seriously to ensure the safety of staff and clients. This approach is realized through a hierarchy of lobbies and private spaces that provide a comfortable space for victims. Children and their families receive a similar experience tailored in a playful environment. In addition, concealed corridors allow minimal passage of staff through private spaces. The concealed spaces, as well as shared amenities, facilitate a collaborative environment among staff and external agencies. For emergency residency, shared living and dining spaces surround a centralized reception desk that maximizes views of the shelter. The desk's position allows staff to work closely with victims and ensure a safe, welcoming environment. Flexible spaces accommodate single residents and families, with rooms for privacy and social interaction. Access to a secure playground, fitness center, chapel, and childcare creates a smooth transition to the community environment.

Sojourner Family Peace Center's strategic placement in a predominantly Black neighborhood is a safe haven for an at-risk community. A 2010 CDC survey revealed 43.7% of Black women have experienced rape, physical violence, or stalking by an intimate partner in their lifetime. The percentage is significantly higher than White (34.6%) and Latino (37.1%) women. Many factors contribute to violence against Black women, including poverty, drug and alcohol use, and sex trafficking. When seeking help, many victims remain silent over their distrust of police, biased justice systems, and fears of retaliation. The Sojourner Family Peace Center hopes to reduce these factors and barriers through its services, in turn encouraging Black women (and all victims of abuse) to speak out, survive, and reduce domestic violence. With nearly 600 women and children assisted annually, the facility's singular point of service helps victims re-establish their lives and build stronger communities.

Selected Accolades: Real Estate Project of the Year - Milwaukee Business Journal (2015)

ST. PHILIP'S EPISCOPAL CHURCH

VERTNER WOODSON TANDY and GEORGE WASHINGTON FOSTER *(Tandy & Foster)*
New York City, NY (1910)

St. Philip's Episcopal Church was formed out of racial tension within the historic Trinity Church. African American worshipers, longing for the end of slavery, migrated from their century-old sanctuary and established the Free African Church of St. Philip in 1809. The congregation consisted of free persons and slaves and served as a forerunner in religious and social welfare. In 1818, the foundation was laid for St. Philip's Episcopal Church in Lower Manhattan.

Over the next 90 years, the church experienced much hardship. The new church of the congregation, constructed of wood, burned down in 1822 and was replaced by a stone structure. Twelve years later, a mob of 300 angry White residents vandalized the church and its furnishings, prompting reconstruction. The New York Draft Riots (1863) caused the building to be used as barracks for militia and police officers handling the riots, again damaging the structure. St. Philip's Episcopal Church relocated in 1857 and 1886 before settling at its present home in Harlem. The present church is designed in a Neo-Gothic architectural style, with entries on both ends of the main facade. Its interior is finished with exposed Roman brick, unlike other churches in the early 20th century that were covered in painted plaster. Marble trim lines terrazzo aisles and chancel floors, an aesthetic often found in well-designed churches. St. Philip's elegance is owed to the team of Vertner Woodson Tandy and George Washington Foster, who respectively were the first licensed African American architects in New York and among the first in New Jersey. Tandy was also a member of the congregation.

The church's permanent home in Harlem ushered in a wave of success for its congregation and community.

St. Philip's quickly rose to prominence, boasting such members as W. E. B. Du Bois, Thurgood Marshall, and Langston Hughes. Numerous amenities managed by the church uplifted the African American population, including a credit union (1951), community center (1970), and housing projects. In the 1960s and 70s, many of the church's properties were renovated by the Black architects Henri A. LeGendre and Percy Ifill, as part of a mission to employ African American businesses. In addition to addressing social issues, St. Philip's extensively promotes cultural activities, in the form of theater, music, and art. Though much of its congregation has dwindled since the Civil Rights era, the church continues to play an active role in social and civil affairs and remains an integral part of the Harlem community.

Selected Accolades: Designated Landmark - New York City (1993)

STUYVESANT TOWN

*BEVERLY LORAINE GREENE, *Irwan Clavan, Gilmore D. Clarke*
New York City, NY (1947)

Infamous Modern architect Le Corbusier never designed a building in New York, though his influence is exhibited across the city. Disappointed by his lack of opportunities, he criticized the city's lack of harmony among buildings. Corbusier believed New York could benefit from having structures that "don't try to outdo each other but are all identical.[1]" Stuyvesant Town (commonly referred to as Stuy Town) emulates this notion by containing 110 red brick buildings sprawled over 18 city blocks. Much of the space is covered by greenery, as residences occupy only 25% of the site. Each building is connected by winding and landscaped paths, creating a suburban feel in a dense urban environment.

The mastermind behind Stuy Town was Robert Moses, the 'Master Builder[2]' of New York's infrastructure boom during the early to mid-twentieth century. Despite not holding an elected position, Moses was responsible for 150,000 housing units. A large number of units were placed in 'blighted' areas, which were despised by Moses. The grounds of Stuy Town displaced a disproportionate amount of minorities, including Blacks, in what previously was known as the Gashouse District. 11,000 citizens were forced to vacate their homes, through the removal of hundreds of homes, shops, schools, and churches. Stuy Town was built devoid of these community buildings, much to the dismay of many residents, and lawsuits filed against Metropolitan Life (the owner of the complex) were unheard by the U.S. Supreme Court on the basis of private financing.

Metropolitan Life (MetLife) also barred Blacks from renting, as its president feared a mix of African American residents would decrease Stuy Town's value. Beginning in 1948, a series of tactics to combat discrimination led to activists temporarily housing a Black family, who eventually succeeded despite jobs losses and threats of evictions.

By 1950, social pressure forced MetLife to allow three Black families to live in the complex, much to the relief of many residents.

Beverly Loraine Greene, often recognized as the woman behind the 80-acre Stuy Town, only worked on the project for a few days before accepting a scholarship to Columbia University.

Though she is recognized as the first documented African American female architect in the United States it is quite remarkable that Greene was even chosen for the project, due to MetLife's racist practices. Once desegregation occurred three years after Stuy Town's completion, a diverse environment gradually progressed. Over the years, tenants shifted from middle class families to privileged college and postgraduate students; however, Stuy Town, along with its sister development Peter Cooper Village, offer a lottery for lower-income families to maintain a diverse community in its unique environment.

[1] Schulz, Dana. 2014. (p.103); [2] Sarachan, Sydney. 2013. (p.103)

SUGAR HILL DEVELOPMENT

DAVID ADJAYE *(Adjaye Associates), SLCE Architects*
New York City, NY (2014)

Sugar Hill Development, located in the famed black neighborhood of Harlem, aims to reduce poverty and revitalize the historic district. The development includes affordable housing (with housing for the homeless), a pre-school, and a museum. Sugar Hill is hailed as a new typology in housing, as it aims to incorporate a sense of community with its living and educational components.

The 191,000 square foot complex is designed to integrate within the context of the community. Surrounded by Gothic Revival row houses, Sugar Hill acknowledges their presence by abstractly referencing the masonry ornament and row house bays. Graphite colored, precast concrete panels of the facade sparkle in sunlight, allowing the building to shimmer throughout the day. The color of the panels also starkly contrasts the glass facade that wraps around the entire building. Several terraces frame significant New York landmarks, such as Central Park, One World Trade Center, and Yankee Stadium.

Sugar Hill was conceived by Broadway Housing Communities (BHC), who served as the catalyst for the educational and cultural heart of the complex. The Sugar Hill Children's Museum of Art and Storytelling serves the historic neighborhood by educating families on local and global interests through inter-generational dialogue with artists, art, and storytelling. Children also have the opportunity to have their voice heard by creating art and stories of their own. BHC's commitment to the museum has given Sugar Hill's residents and community the stimulation to address income, education, and cultural awareness issues that are often prevalent. Through its successful mixture of programs, Sugar Hill aims to become a new symbol of civic pride and valuable resource within Harlem.

Selected Accolades: Design Award - AIA New York (2016)

THEME BUILDING

*PAUL WILLIAMS *(Welton Becket and Associates), Pereira & Luckman and Associates*
Los Angeles, CA (1961)

Contrary to popular belief, the Theme Building at Los Angeles International Airport (LAX) was not designed by Paul Williams. He did, however, work for the firm Welton Becket, responsible for the design. How was Williams pinned as the architect? The mistaken credit stems from America's attempt to promote diversity internationally. Julius Shulman, a well-known photographer, captured Williams in 1965 at the front of the Theme Building. The photo was used by the United States Information Agency, as a response to the Mutual Educational and Cultural Exchange Act of 1961, to prove to other nations the U.S. was a diverse, inclusive democracy. It's ironic that the act was passed in the midst of the Civil Rights Movement. Williams attempted to discredit his design involvement; however, word quickly spread that he was the architect of record. It is important to note that Williams' accidental accreditation of the Theme Building is one of the rare instances an African American architect is credited with the work of their White counterpart.

Regardless of the structure's architect, the Theme Building has become an iconic symbol of Los Angeles. Its original intent was to house a main ticketing entry with a glass dome connected to terminals. Those plans never came to fruition, and the building stands alone outside of airport security. The building is composed of two spider-like stucco covered arches that support a 'saucer' pavilion, formerly home to a space-age restaurant that is accessible through the building's core. Surrounding the building is a circular concrete wall, playfully hiding the base of the landmark. The futuristic structure is a shift from Los Angeles's traditional Beaux Arts style of building, signifying a progression towards a modern future.

In 2010, the Theme Building underwent a seismic retrofitting after the collapse of stucco. The Encounter Restaurant, a staple of the building, closed its doors in 2014 after 17 years of operation. The Theme Building, however, continues to offer rooftop access free to the general public. While business operations have faced uncertainty, officials recognize the popularity of the structure and vow to leave the exterior untouched. In spring of 2018, LAX's Bob Hope USO center relocated to the ground floor, adding new life and use to the facility. The Theme Building continues to display its Googie style pavilion and is remembered as a forerunner in the Modern Los Angeles architecture movement.

Selected Accolades: Los Angeles Historic Cultural Monument (1993)

TUSKEGEE UNIVERSITY CHAPEL

ROBERT R. TAYLOR
LOUIS FRY and JOHN A. WELCH *(Fry and Welch), Paul Rudolph*
Tuskegee, AL (1898 & 1969)

Though not a religious institution, Tuskegee University made spiritual activities an integral part of the early campus. Religious services, as well as ceremonies and conferences, were held in the Pavilion, an 1880s structure designed as a makeshift glorified shed. The Pavilion faced much scrutiny and often leaked on its occupants. In 1895, under the university's leader and founder Booker T. Washington, funds for a chapel were acquired through the generosity of the Stokes sisters. Washington suggested Robert R. Taylor for the chapel's design, a move that proved beneficial to the campus, as dozens of additional buildings were designed under Taylor's hand.

Minor pullback and simplistic design revisions from the Stokes sisters positioned the chapel away from the main portion of campus. Its quiet location provided a solemn procession for students and faculty. The building contained 1,200,000 bricks produced by forty students from a local brickyard. Students also aided in the design of pews and cornices. The chapel's plan was a Greek cross, symmetrical in appearance except for a 105-foot tower, and was the first building in Alabama to use interior electrical lights. With much praise from Washington and the media, the chapel stood as one of the few places where Blacks and Whites revered God together in religious activities.

In 1957, lightning struck the roof of the chapel, causing the building to burn down. Twelve years later, a new building was erected, in part by former Tuskegee faculty Louis Fry and John A. Welch. The new chapel is praised for its dramatic facade and inspiring sanctuary, both of which are free of right angles. Its parabolic roof is ideal for acoustics, and slits along its edges provide ample natural light. The chapel is also known for its stained glass 'Singing Windows[1],' previously installed in a 1932 renovation, depicting eleven popular Negro spirituals, paying homage to the former building. For more than a century, distinguished guests (including Mary McLeod Bethune, Martin Luther King Jr., and U.S. presidents) have visited the chapel as it continues to serve the religious needs of Tuskegee University.

[1] "History of the Chapel." (pg.100)

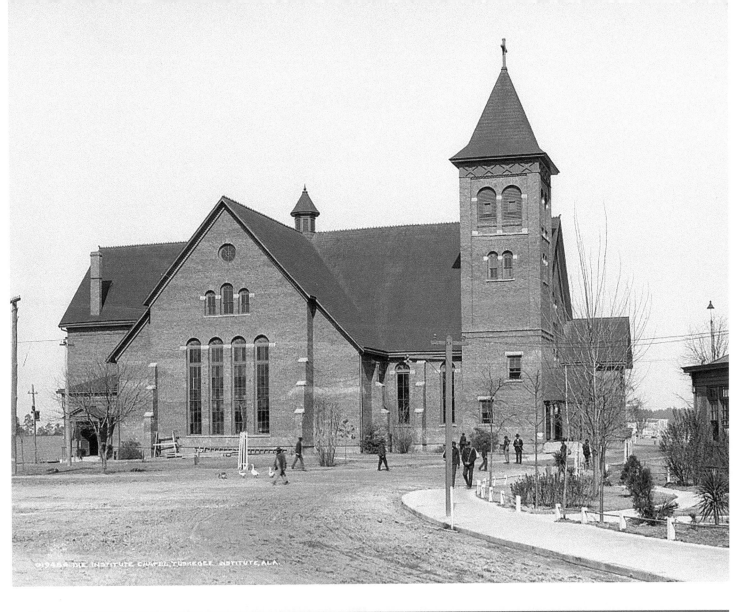

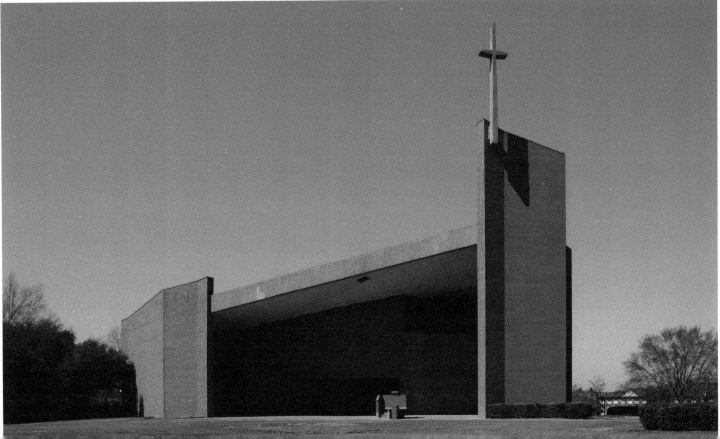

VILLA LEWARO

VERTNER WOODSON TANDY
Irvington, NY (1918)

Villa Lewaro is most famous for its first occupant, Madame C.J. Walker. Born in mid-1800s Louisiana as the daughter of slaves, Walker worked to build a successful hair product empire. Her business earned her the recognition of being one of America's first female self-made millionaires.

The early twentieth century brought on the Harlem Renaissance, propelling Walker to move closer to the African American cultural capital. In 1915, Walker commissioned New York's first Black registered architect, Vertner Woodson Tandy, to design a townhouse. A year later, Walker again hired Tandy to complete her dream of owning a suburban estate. The estate was intended as a representation of prestige and success for all African Americans. Located in a predominantly White neighborhood, the home's intention of demonstrating the achievement of Black wealth proved inspirational for future generations.

Walker's home was named "Villa Lewaro," stemming from two letters of her daughter's names, A'Lelia Walker Robinson. The 20,000 square foot home encompasses thirty rooms, filled with gold leaf Corinthian columns, hand-painted ceilings, and spectacular stained glass windows. Its ornate Italian Renaissance Revival design emphasizes prosperity and wealth. In tune with her past, Walker provided windows for her servants (who were Black), contrary to custom during the early 20th century. Well after Villa Lewaro's completion, the estate was recognized as "the finest home ever owned by a Negro.[1]" Walker's passion for Black advancement often led to lavish social and cultural events. The family was well known for hosting exquisite parties, drawing the likes of several famous African Americans, including Marcus Garvey, W.E.B. Dubois, Zora Neale Hurston, and Langston Hughes.

Walker's life in Villa Lewaro was short-lived, as she passed away in 1919. A'Lelia Robinson maintained the estate until her death in 1931. The property changed to a retirement home through the 1970s, until becoming a private residence. Dedication by the estate's current owners has preserved and restored the mansion to its original grandeur, and a movement is underway to have the estate more accessible to the public.

Selected Accolades: National Register of Historic Places (1976)

[1] Dixon, Kathy. 2014. (p.98)

WEEKSVILLE HERITAGE CENTER

EVERARDO JEFFERSON *(Caples Jefferson Architects)*
New York City, NY (2013)

Weeksville Heritage Center stems from the 19th-century settlement of Weeksville, a free Black society in Brooklyn. The town was founded in 1838 following the abolishment of slavery in New York State. Weeksville quickly became a haven for African Americans escaping the New York Draft Riots and southerners fleeing slavery. By 1850, the settlement was the second largest community of free Blacks in the United States. The community not only provided a chance for Blacks in prestigious fields (doctors, businessmen, etc.) to achieve success, but the town also fostered an active abolitionist movement. At the turn of the century, Weeksville was home to more than 500 families who lived in a thriving society.

The early 1900s marked the downfall of Weeksville, spurred by urban renewal. Much of the settlement was lost until rediscovered in 1968 by James Hurley and Joseph Haynes. Their efforts saved four wooden cottages, which are the only remnants of the town from the 19th century. The homes successfully survived a demolition attempt and gained national attention in the 1970s. In 2005, the cottages were fully restored and made available for public tours.

Following restoration, a facility to educate and preserve the past community of Weeksville was completed. Weeksville Heritage Center aims to "document, preserve, and interpret[1]" by offering visitors glimpses into the lives of past African Americans. In addition to a museum, the new complex contains exhibition space, workshops, classrooms, a library, and performance space. The 23,000 square foot center utilizes subtle West African themes, particularly in the wood and frit glass designs, to strengthen the heritage of the site. The L-shaped composition creates a physical and imaginary boundary that diagonally connects to the cottages, along a former Native American trail. Weeksville Heritage Center's contemporary design perfectly contrasts alongside the cottages of the mid-19th century, creating an ideal environment for engaging in the settlement's past.

Selected Accolades: LEED Gold, Honor Award - NOMA (2013), Best of New York - AIA New York (2014), COTE Sustainability Institutional Award - AIA New York (2015)

[1] "What We Do." (pg.104)

BIBLIOGRAPHY

"About The Center." *The Harvey B. Gantt Center for African-American Arts + Culture,* http://www.ganttcenter.org/about-the-center/

"About the Memorial." *Washington, DC Martin Luther King, Jr. National Memorial Project Foundation,* https://web.archive.org/web/20110919131236/http://www.mlkmemorial.org/site/c.hkIUL9MVJxE/b.7548975/k.9356/Site_Location.htm.

"About the Schomburg Center for Research in Black Culture." *The New York Public Library,* https://www.nypl.org/about/locations/schomburg.

"About Us." *Center for Civil and Human Rights,* https://www.civilandhumanrights.org/about-us/.

"About Us." *Houston Public Library,* 12 Sept. 2018, houstonlibrary.org/research/special-collections/african-american-library-gregory-school/about-us.

Ackerman, Lauren. "DuSable Museum of African American History (1961–)." *Black Past,* blackpast.org/aah/dusable-museum-african-american-history-1961.

"Adam Clayton Powell Building." *NYC Urbanism,* 8 May 2017, www.nycurbanism.com/brutalnyc/2017/2/8/adam-clayton-powell-building.

"The Adam Clayton Powell, Jr. State Office Building." *Institute for Religion, Culture, and Public Life,* 3 Feb. 2011, ircpl.columbia.edu/2011/02/03/the-adam-clayton-powell-jr-state-office-building/.

Adler, Eric, and Aaron Randle. "The New 'East of Troost': Chef's Kitchens, Lap Pools, $600K Homes - and Class Tension." *The Kansas City Star,* 5 Oct. 2017, www.kansascity.com/news/business/development/article177276366.html.

"African American Civil War Memorial." *DP + Partners,* www.dppartnersarchitects.com/african-american-civil-war-memorial.html.

"African American Civil War Museum." Jair Lynch Real Estate Partners, www.jairlynch.com/projects/african-american-civil-war-museum-4/.

"African Burial Ground Interpretive Center." *Amaze Design,* www.amazedesign.com/#/african-burial-ground-interpretive-center/.

"African Burial Ground Interpretive Center." *Roberta Washington Architects,* www.robertawashington.com/cultural_commercial/african-burial-ground-interpretive-center/.

"African Burial Ground Memorial, New York, NY." *U.S. General Services Administration,* 13 Aug. 2017, www.gsa.gov/historic-buildings/african-burial-ground-memorial-new-york-ny.

"Asem-Pa." *Adjaye Associates,* http://www.adjaye.com/projects/residential/asem-pa-make-it-right/.

Ashaboglu, Selin. "Francis A. Gregory Neighborhood Library." *Architect Magazine,* 25 Sept. 2015, www.architectmagazine.com/project-gallery/francis-a-gregory-neighborhood-library_o.

"August Wilson Center for African American Culture / Perkins+Will." *ArchDaily,* 28 Aug. 2011, www.archdaily.com/163047/august-wilson-center-for-african-american-culture-perkinswill. "August Wilson Center Wins AIA Pittsburgh Award." *Perkins+Will*, 6 Feb. 2015, perkinswill.com/news/august-wilson-center-wins-aia-pittsburgh-award.html.

Bagli, Charles V. "A New Light on a Fight to Integrate Stuyvesant Town." *The New York Times*, 21 Nov. 2010, https://www.nytimes.com/2010/11/22/nyregion/22stuyvesant.html.

Baird-Remba, Rebecca. "Harlem's 125th Street Is Going 'to Look like 34th Street' Next Year." *Commercial Observer*, 13 Apr. 2017, commercialobserver.com/2017/04/harlem-125th-street-big-chains-columbia-manhattanville/.

Barnes, Michael. "Tour lauds Austin midcentury design pathfinder John Chase." *Austin American-Statesman*, 15 Sep. 2018, https://www.statesman.com/NEWS/20131004/Tour-lauds-Austin-midcentury-design-pathfinder-John-Chase.

"Beacon Hill - Kansas City, MO." *Pendulum*, www.pendulumkc.com/portfolio/#/beacon-hill/.

"Beacon Hill." *Urban Neighborhood Initiative*, uni-kc.org/neighborhoods/beacon-hill/.

"Berkley Square Historic District, Las Vegas, Nevada." *The Paul Revere Williams Project,* www.paulrwilliamsproject.org/gallery/berkley-square-historic-district-las-vegas-nevada/.

Bey, Lee. "Cool Building Wednesday: Ebony-Jet Building." *WBEZ 91.5 Chicago,* 21 Apr. 2010, https://www.wbez.org/shows/wbez-news/cool-building-wednesday-ebony-jet-building/181d6a98-2f6d-4552-bae0-19f4b2741e19.

Bey, Lee. "Soul survivor: A look at the intact and avant garde interiors of the Ebony/Jet Building." *WBEZ 91.5 Chicago*, 14 Jan. 2013, https://www.wbez.org/shows/wbez-blogs/soul-survivor-a-look-at-the-intact-and-avant-garde-interiors-of-the-ebonyjet-building/57a4ad24-f4aa-4653-8439-9aa99df0fb22.

"Birmingham Church Bombing." *History*, https://www.history.com/topics/black-history/birmingham-church-bombing-video.

Bloom, Elizabeth. "The Rise and Fall of the August Wilson Center." *Pittsburgh Post-Gazette,* 8 Feb. 2014, www.post-gazette.com/ae/theater-dance/2014/02/09/Rise-and-fall-of-August-Wilson-Center/stories/201402090045.

Boese, Kent. "Howard Theatre: A history." *Greater Greater Washington*, 20 May 2009, https://ggwash.org/view/1866/howard-theatre-a-history

"Booker T. Washington." *Biography*, 1 Mar. 2018, www.biography.com/people/booker-t-washington-9524663.

Bowsher, Alice M. "Sixteenth Street Baptist Church." *SAH Archipedia*, https://sah-archipedia.org/buildings/AL-01-073-0050.

Brinlee, Morgan. "More Black Women Are Killed In America Than Any Other Race, A New CDC Report Says." *Bustle*, 22 July 2017, https://www.bustle.com/p/more-black-women-are-killed-in-america-than-any-other-race-a-new-cdc-report-says-71955.

Bryce, Mary. "Full of Light." *East*, 30 May 2017, http://www.eastsideatx.com/john-chase-architecture/.

"The Building." Duke University Chapel, chapel.duke.edu/mission/building.
"The Building." *National Museum of African American History & Culture*, https://nmaahc.si.edu/explore/building.

"Built By Women: Peter Cooper Village – Stuyvesant Town, Beverly Loraine Greene." *Beverly Willis Architecture Foundation,* 26 Feb. 2014, https://web.archive.org/web/20151030065507/http://www.bwaf.org/built-by-women-peter-cooper-village-stuyvesant-town-beverly-loraine-greene/.

Catron, Derek. "Suits Were Not The First The Adam's Mark In St. Louis Was The Focus Of Two Other Cases During The 1990s, And There Have Been Controversies At Other Properties In The 23-Hotel Luxury

Chain." *Orlando Sentinel*, 22 Mar. 2000, articles. orlandosentinel.com/2000-03-22/news/0003220079_1_kummer-adam-discrimination.

"Chapel, Tuskegee Institute, Tuskegee AL, 1958-1969." *Paul Rudolph & His Architecture*, http://prudolph.lib.umassd.edu/node/4729. "Chapter 33 - Mutual Education and Cultural Exchange Program." *United States Code*, http://uscode.house.gov/view.xhtml?path=/prelim@title22/chapter33&edition=prelim.

"Charles H. Wright Museum of African American History." *Historic Detroit*, www.historicdetroit.org/building/charles-h-wright-museum-of-african-american-history/.

"Choice Neighborhoods Initiative: Iberville-Tremé." *Concordia*, http://concordia.com/projects/iberville-choice-neighborhoods/.

Cholke, Sam. "DuSable Museum Boss Wants Burnham's Roundhouse Open Before Obama Center." *DNAinfo*, 8 Sept. 2017, www.dnainfo.com/chicago/20170905/hyde-park/dusable-museum-of-african-american-history-roundhouse-daniel-burnham-president-barack-obama-library-center/.

Clark, Josh. "What's a shotgun house?" *How Stuff Works*, 19 May 2009, https://home.howstuffworks.com/home-improvement/construction/planning/shotgun-house.htm.

Cooper, Rachel. "Visit the African American Civil War Memorial and Museum." *Trip Savvy*, 13 Aug. 2018, www.tripsavvy.com/african-american-civil-war-memorial-and-museum-1039268.

Cope, Donna. "Live the Legacy: Visit Booker T. Washington's Mansion at Tuskegee." *Alabama NewsCenter*, 17 Feb. 2017, alabamanewscenter.com/2017/02/17/booker-t-washington-legacy-lives-on-at-tuskegee-university-with-25000-visits-yearly/.

Corda, Simone. "Weeksville Heritage Center." *Caples Jefferson Architects*, http://www.capjeff.com/weeksville-heritage-center.

"Cradle to Cradle." *Make It Right*, http://makeitright.org/c2c/.

Crumlic, William. "St. Philip's Episcopal Church - Architecture and History." *Youtube*, narrated by Mark G. Barksdale, 11 Apr. 2010, https://www.youtube.com/watch?v=e6QnliwQuIo.

D'Oyley, Demetria L. "Madam C.J. Walker's Restored Estate Recaptures a Grand History." *The Root*, 03 Sep. 2014, https://www.theroot.com/madam-c-j-walker-s-restored-estate-recaptures-a-grand-1790876899.

"David Adjaye's Sugar Hill Development: A New Typology for Affordable Housing." *ArchDaily*, 11 June, 2014, https://www.archdaily.com/514785/david-adjaye-s-sugar-hill-development-a-new-typology-for-affordable-housing.

Dixon, John M. "Weeksville Heritage Center, Designed by Caples Jefferson Architects." *Architect Magazine*, 17 Oct. 2013, https://www.architectmagazine.com/design/buildings/weeksville-heritage-center-designed-by-caples-jefferson-architects_o.

Dixon, Kathy. ""A Sort of Monument": Why Villa Lewaro Is More Than a Building." *Huffpost*, 23 Oct. 2014, https://www.huffingtonpost.com/national-trust-for-historic-preservation/a-sort-of-monument-why-vi_b_6035962.html.

Duke, Lynne. "Blueprint of a Life." *Washington Post*, 07 July 2004, http://www.washingtonpost.com/wp-dyn/articles/A19414-2004Jun30.html.

"Duke's Architecture." *Duke University*, fmd.duke.edu/campus/architecture/index.php.

"Dunbar High School, Washington DC." *NOMA*, 17 Feb. 2015, http://www.noma.net/article/240/happenings/spotlight/featured-project/dunbar-high-school-washington-dc.

Dunlap, David W. "History Finally Finds the State Office Building on 125th Street." *The New York Times*, 5 Nov. 2008, www.nytimes.com/2008/11/06/nyregion/

06thennow.html.

Durden, Robert F. "Duke University." *NCpedia*, 2006, www.ncpedia.org/duke-university.

Dutton, Thomas A., and Lian Hurst Mann. *Reconstructing Architecture: Critical Discourses and Social Practices*. University of Minnesota Press, 2010.

Ferola, Anne. "Saving the August Wilson Center." *Nonprofit Quarterly*, 26 Feb. 2016, nonprofitquarterly.org/2016/01/20/saving-the-august-wilson-center/.Firestone, Rebecca. "New Orleans Post-Katrina: Making It Right?" *The Architect's Take*, 25 Jan. 2011, https://thearchitectstake.com/editorials/new-orleans-post-katrina-making-right/.

"First African Methodist Episcopal Church." *Los Angeles Conservancy*, www.laconservancy.org/locations/first-african-methodist-episcopal-church.

"First AME Church, Los Angeles, CA." *The Paul Revere Williams Project*, www.paulrwilliamsproject.org/gallery/first-ame-church-los-angeles-ca/.

"Fisk University Master Plan." *City of Nashville*, 27 Oct. 2008, https://www.nashville.gov/Portals/0/SiteContent/Planning/docs/urban/Institutional%20Overlays/fisk.pdf.

Forgione, Mary. "LAX Theme Building will house USO center starting in spring 2018." *LA Times*, 19 Dec. 2017, http://www.latimes.com/travel/deals/la-tr-lax-theme-building-will-gain-uso-center-in-2018-story.html.

"Francis A. Gregory Library History." *DC Public Library*, https://www.dclibrary.org/node/724.

Gambino, Megan. "Building the Martin Luther King, Jr. National Memorial." *Smithsonian Magazine*, 18 Aug. 2011, https://www.smithsonianmag.com/history/building-the-martin-luther-king-jr-national-memorial-54721785/.

Gerfen, Katie. "National Center for Civil and Human Rights." *Architect Magazine*, 11 May 2015, https://www.architectmagazine.com/project-gallery/national-center-for-civil-and-human-rights.

Goodyear, Dana. "Hotel California." *The New Yorker*, 07 Feb. 2005, https://www.newyorker.com/magazine/2005/02/07/hotel-california.

Gordy, Cynthia. "The MLK Memorial's Complicated History." *The Root*, 22 Aug. 2011, https://www.theroot.com/the-mlk-memorials-complicated-history-1790865442.

Gratz, Roberta B. "Who Killed Public Housing in New Orleans?" *The Nation*, 02 June 2015, https://www.thenation.com/article/requiem-bricks/.

Hanc, John. "Birmingham's Civil Rights Institute Personalizes a Struggle." *The New York Times*, 14 Mar. 2012, www.nytimes.com/2012/03/15/arts/artsspecial/birmingham-civil-rights-institute-personalizes-a-struggle.html?_r=1&pagewanted=all.

"Harold Varner (Aug. 22, 1935 - Dec. 14, 2013)." *Historic Detroit*, historicdetroit.org/architect/harold-varner/.

Harrison, Scott. "How LAX's Theme Building became an iconic symbol of Los Angeles." *LA Times*, 26 Nov. 2015, http://www.latimes.com/local/california/la-me-retrospective-lax-20151126-story.html.

"Harvey B Gantt Center for African-American Arts + Culture." *Perkins + Will*, https://perkinswill.com/work/harvey-b-gantt-center-african-american-arts-culture.

Herman, Valli. "A look at the L.A.-themed makeover at LAX's Terminal 6." *LA Times*, 24 Oct. 2016, http://www.latimes.com/travel/deals/la-tr-lax-terminal-6-renovation-20161021-snap-story.html.

Hintz, Eric S. "An Early Attempt to Build a "National Museum for Colored People." *Lemelson Center*, 15 Sep. 2016, http://invention.si.edu/early-attempt-build-national-museum-colored-people.

"Historic - Cultural Monuments (HCM) Listing." *The City Project*, http://www.cityprojectca. org/ourwork/documents/ HCMDatabase090707.pdf.

"Historical Sketch of Dunbar High School." *Paul Laurence Dunbar Senior High School*, https://www. dunbarhsdc.org/history.html.

"History." *Make It Right*, http:// makeitright.org/about/history/.

"History." *Northeastern University*, https://www.northeastern.edu/aai/ about/history/.

"History & Timeline." *The Memorial Foundation*, http://www. thememorialfoundation.org/history-timeline.

"History of the Chapel." *Tuskegee University*, https://www.tuskegee. edu/about-us/chapel-history.

"History of Tuskegee University." *Tuskegee University*, www.tuskegee. edu/about-us/history-and-mission.

"Houston African American Library and Museum." *Smith & Company Architects*, www.sc-arch.com/african-american-library.

"Howard Theater." *Martinez + Johnson Architecture,* http://www. mjarchitecture.com/howard-theatre/.

"Howard Theater." *Michael Marshall Design,* https:// michaelmarshalldesign.com/project/ howard-theater/.

"The Howard Theatre." *Architect Magazine,* 15 Oct. 2012, https://www. architectmagazine.com/project-gallery/the-howard-theatre.

"Iberville Redevelopment." *HRI Properties*, https://www. hriproperties.com/current-project/ iberville-on-site/.

Jensen, Trevor. "Wendell Campbell: 1927 - 2008." *Chicago Tribune*, 15 July 2008, www.chicagotribune. com/news/ct-xpm-2008-07-15-0807140466-story.html.

"John D. O'Bryant African-American Institute." *Jones Architecture*, http:// www.jonesarch.com/academic-libraries/john-d-obryant-african-american-institute-library/.

"John D. O'Bryant African-American Institute." *Stull and Lee* http:// stullandlee.com/architecture/ john-d-obryant-african-american-institute/.

"John H. Johnson." *Biography*, 25 July 2016, www.biography.com/people/ john-h-johnson-020116.

"John Mercer Langston." *Biography*, 2 Apr. 2014, www.biography. com/people/john-mercer-langston-9373265.

Johnson, Erick. "EBONY magazine moves to Los Angeles." *Amsterdam News*, 31 May 2017, http:// amsterdamnews.com/news/2017/ may/31/ebony-magazine-moves-los-angeles/.

Kass, Mark. "Sojourner Family Peace Center wins top prize in Business Journal's 2016 Real Estate Awards: See all the winners." *Milwaukee Business Journal*, 14 Apr. 2016, https://www.bizjournals.com/ milwaukee/news/2016/04/14/see-which-projects-won-the-milwaukee-business.html.

King, Shaun. "Kansas City Hotel Manager Hangs Black Doll from Doorway in Office to Mock Sandra Bland." *Daily Kos*, 28 July 2015, www.dailykos.com/ stories/2015/07/28/1406527/-Kansas-City-hotel-manager-hangs-black-doll-from-doorway-in-office-to-mock-Sandra-Bland.

King, William E. "Duke University: A Brief Narrative History." *Duke University Libraries*, 29 Oct. 2018, library.duke.edu/rubenstein/ uarchives/history/articles/narrative-history.

Kissinger, Michael. "St. Philip's Protestant Episcopal Church, New York City (1809-)." *Black Past*, https://blackpast.org/aah/st-philip-s-protestant-episcopal-church-new-york-city-1809.

Kozlarz, Jay. "Apartment conversion of Chicago's Johnson Publishing Building moves forward." *Curbed Chicago*, 28 Nov. 2017, https://chicago.curbed. com/2017/11/28/16704350/south-loop-johnson-publishing-apartment-conversion.

"Langston Terrace Dwellings/Hilyard Robinson, African American Heritage Trail." *Cultural Tourism DC*, https://www.culturaltourismdc.org/portal/langston-terrace-dwellings/hilyard-robinson-african-american-heritage-trail.

"Langston Terrace, Washington, D.C." *The Paul Revere Williams Project*, http://www.paulrwilliamsproject.org/gallery/langston-terrace-washington-dc/.

"A Legacy of Firsts: Texas Architect John S. Chase." *Humanities Texas*, Feb. 2018, https://www.humanitiestexas.org/news/articles/legacy-firsts-texas-architect-john-s-chase.

"Library History-Fisk University Library, Nashville, Tennessee." *Pastures of Plenty*, 14 May 2011, pasturesoplenty.wordpress.com/2011/05/08/library-history-fisk-university-library-nashville-tennessee/.

"Los Angeles International Airport." *The Paul Revere Williams Project*, http://www.paulrwilliamsproject.org/gallery/1960s-transportation/.

Luthern, Ashley. "'Accountable': Are domestic violence victims in Milwaukee getting the help they need?" *Milwaukee Journal Sentinel*, 04 Apr. 2018, https://www.jsonline.com/story/news/local/milwaukee/2018/04/04/accountable-domestic-violence-victims-milwaukee-getting-help-they-need/467352002/.

Luthern, Ashley. "Two years after opening new facility for domestic abuse survivors, Sojourner Family Peace Center keeps growing." *Milwaukee Journal Sentinel*, 09 Nov. 2017, https://www.jsonline.com/story/news/local/milwaukee/2017/11/09/two-years-after-opening-new-center-domestic-abuse-survivors-sojourner-family-peace-center-keeps-grow/834402001/.

Lyle, Michael. "Discover the Trail of Black History in Las Vegas." *Las Vegas Review-Journal*, 2 Mar. 2017, www.reviewjournal.com/life/discover-the-trail-of-black-history-in-las-vegas/. "Make It Right Homes." Billes Partners, http://www.billespartners.com/pages/portfolio/default.aspx?catid=3&projectid=50.

Mackel, Travers. "Brad Pitt 'Make It Right' homes riddled with problems, say some residents." *WSDU News*, 19 Apr. 2018, https://www.wdsu.com/article/brad-pitt-make-it-right-homes-riddled-with-problems-say-some-residents/19864373.

"Martin Luther King, Jr. Memorial." McKissack McKissack, https://www.mckinc.com/project/martin-luther-king-jr-memorial.

"Memorial & Museum History." *African American Civil War Museum*, afroamcivilwar.org/about-us/memorial-museum-history.html.

"Mission and History." *Northeastern University*, https://www.northeastern.edu/aai/about/mission-and-history/.

Mom0ja. "The Oaks." *Atlas Obscura*, 15 Jan. 2016, www.atlasobscura.com/places/the-oaks-tuskegee-alabama.

"Myers Street School." *The Charlotte-Mecklenburg Story*, https://www.cmstory.org/exhibits/african-american-album-volume-2-places/myers-street-school.

"National Center for Civil and Human Rights / HOK + The Freelon Group (Now part of Perkins+Will)." *ArchDaily*, 22 July 2015, https://www.archdaily.com/770551/national-center-for-civil-and-human-rights-the-freelon-group-architects-plus-hok.

"National Center for Civil and Human Rights." *AIA Georgia*, https://www.aiaga.org/design-award/national-center-for-civil-and-human-rights/.

"National Center for Civil and Human Rights." *AIA North Carolina*, 1 Oct. 2015, http://www.aiancawards.org/national-center-for-civil-and-human-rights/.

"National Center for Civil and Human Rights." *Perkins + Will*, https://perkinswill.com/work/national-center-civil-and-human-rights.

"National Intimate Partner and Sexual Violence Survey." *Centers for Disease Control and Prevention*, 2010, https://www.cdc.gov/violenceprevention/pdf/nisvs_report2010-a.pdf.

"National Museum of African American History & Culture." *Clark Construction*, https://www.clarkconstruction.com/our-work/projects/national-museum-african-american-history-culture.

"National Register of Historic Places Program." *National Park Service*, https://www.nps.gov/nr/feature/places/14000692.htm.

"National Register of Historic Places." *Texas Historical Commission*, www.thc.texas.gov/preserve/projects-and-programs/national-register-historic-places.

"New Academic Center and Freshman Honors Program at Northeastern University." *William Rawn Associates*, http://www.rawnarch.com/sites/default/files/projectfiles/Northeastern-University-Building-F.pdf.

"New Deal." *History*, 14 Sep. 2018, https://www.history.com/topics/great-depression/new-deal.

"The New Granada Theater Listed on National Register of Historic Places." *Pittsburgh History & Landmarks Foundation*, 28 Jan 2011, https://phlf.org/2011/01/28/the-new-granada-theater-listed-on-national-register-

of-historic-places/.

"News Releases." *Hyatt Newsroom*, 8 Feb. 2008, newsroom.hyatt.com/2008-02-08-Adam-s-Mark-St-Louis-to-Become-Hyatt-Regency-St-Louis-Riverfront.

"Our Story." *Sugar Hill Children's Museum of Art & Storytelling*, https://www.sugarhillmuseum.org/story/.

"Overview." *Charles H. Wright Museum of African American History*, thewright.org/index.php/explore/about-the-museum/overview-history.

P., Amber. "Martin Luther King Jr. Memorial / ROMA Design Group." *ArchDaily*, 16 Jan. 2012, https://www.archdaily.com/200438/martin-luther-king-jr-memorial-roma-design-group.

"Parcel Detail." *Los Angeles County Assessor*, portal.assessor.lacounty.gov/parceldetail/5058018029.

"Paul L. Dunbar High School." *Moody Nolan*, http://moodynolan.com/portfolio/dc-public-schools-dgs-dunbar-high-school/.

"Paul Williams: Architect to the Stars." *Discover Los Angeles*, 12 Feb. 2008, www.discoverlosangeles.com/blog/paul-williams-architect-stars.

"Pierce Building." *Built St. Louis*, www.builtstlouis.net/opos/piercebuilding.html.

Rhodes, Dawn, and Dahleen Glanton. "DuSable Museum Braces for Change Ahead of Obama Library Arrival." *Chicago Tribune*, 13 Aug. 2015, www.chicagotribune.com/news/local/breaking/ct-dusable-museum-future-met-0814-20150813-story.html.

Riley, Chloe. "Why a Historic Daniel Burnham Building Sits Empty on Chicago's South Side." *WTTW News*, 7 Mar. 2016, news.wttw.com/2016/03/07/why-historic-daniel-burnham-building-sits-empty-chicago-s-south-side.

Rivet, Nathan. "Freedmen's Town, Houston, Texas (1865-)." *Black Past*, blackpast.org/aaw/freedmens-town-houston-texas-1865.

Rixon, Karla. "Paul Laurence Dunbar High School (1870-)." *Black Past*, https://blackpast.org/aah/paul-laurence-dunbar-high-school-1870.

"Rodney Leon Tapped to Design National Historic Landmark; Winner to Create Memorial for 17th, 18th-Century Africans." *Exodus News*, 6 May 2005, web.archive.org/web/20060718042427/http://www.exodusnews.com/HISTORY/History025.htm.

Rosenblum, Charles. "While It Could Have Been More Exciting Architecturally, the New August Wilson Center Connects." *Pittsburgh City Paper*, 8 Nov. 2018, www.pghcitypaper.com/pittsburgh/while-it-could-have-been-more- exciting-architecturally-the-new-august-wilson-center-connects/ Content?oid=1342509.

Rosenburg, Zoe. "In Harlem, NYPL's Schomburg Center Kicks Off $22M Overhaul." *Curbed New York*, 18 Dec. 2015, https://ny.curbed. com/2015/12/18/10852768/in-harlem-nypls-schomburg-center-kicks-off-22m-overhaul.

Rothstein, Edward. "A Burial Ground and Its Dead Are Given Life." *The New York Times*, 26 Feb. 2010, web.archive.org/ web/20100302214226/http://www. nytimes.com/2010/02/26/arts/ design/26burial.html.

Rowley, Erin. "Renovated Samuel E. Kelly Ethnic Cultural Center celebrates grand opening." *University of Washington*, 08 Jan. 2013, https://www.washington.edu/ news/2013/01/08/renovated-samuel-e-kelly-ethnic-cultural-center-celebrates-grand-opening/.

"Samuel E. Kelly Ethnic Cultural Center | University of Washington."*Rolluda Architects*, http://www.rolludaarchitects. com/?p=1684.

Sarachan, Sydney. "The legacy of Robert Moses." *PBS*, 17 Jan. 2013, http://www.pbs.org/wnet/need-to-know/environment/the-legacy-of-robert-moses/16018/.

Saulny, Susan. "Clamoring to Come Home to New Orleans Projects." *The New York Times*,

06 June 2006, https://www. nytimes.com/2006/06/06/us/ nationalspecial/06housing.html.

"Schomburg center opens in New York." *The Afro-American* [New York City] 11 Oct. 1980: 7. Print.

Schulz, Dana. "Towers in the Park: Le Corbusier's Influence in NYC." *6sqft*, 19 Nov. 2014, https://www.6sqft. com/towers-in-the-park-le-corbusiers-influence-in-nyc/.

Scott, Pamela, and Antoinette J. Lee. "Langston Terrace." *SAH Archipedia*, sah-archipedia.org/buildings/DC-01-NE02.

Sinkevitch, Alice, and Laurie McGovern. Petersen. *AIA Guide to Chicago*. University of Illinois Press, 2014.

"Sojourner Family Peace Center." *Mortenson Company*, https:// www.mortenson.com/milwaukee/ projects/sojourner-family-peace-center.

"Sojourner Family Peace Center." *Wisconsin Architect*, http://www. wisconsinarchitect.org/sojournerfpc.

"Sojourner Family Peace Center." *Zimmerman Architectural Studios*, http://www.zastudios.com/project/ sojourner-family-justice-center/.

Solomon, Nancy. *Architecture INTL: Celebrating the Past, Designing the Future*. Harper Design, 2008.

Sorkin, Michael D. "Halevy Simmons Dies; Architect Who Helped Build Adam's Mark Hotel." *STL Today*, 19 Apr. 2013, www.stltoday.com/news/ local/obituaries/halevy-simmons-dies-architect-who-helped-build-adam-s-mark/article_f667753b-4c4d-5aac-85ba-7dfa6c1cdedd.html.

Sowell, Thomas. "Dunbar High School After 100 Years." *Townhall*, 04 Oct. 2016, https:// townhall.com/columnists/ thomassowell/2016/10/04/ dunbar-high-school-after-100-years-n2227261.

"St. Philip's Church records." *The New York Public Library*, http://archives. nypl.org/scm/21156#c1390016.

"St. Philip's Episcopal Church." *The New York City Chapter of the American Guild of Organists*, http:// www.nycago.org/organs/nyc/html/ StPhilipEpis.html.

Stephens, Suzanne. "Francis Gregory Library by Adjaye Associates." *Architectural Record*, 16 Oct. 2012, https://www.architecturalrecord. com/articles/7426-francis-gregory-library-by-adjaye-associates.

Stone, David. *Chicago's Classical Architecture: the Legacy of the White City*. Arcadia, 2005.

"Storyville." *Historical New Orleans*, http://www.storyvilledistrictnola. com/history.html.

"Sugar Hill Housing." *Architect Magazine*, 04 Mar. 2016, https://www.architectmagazine.com/project-gallery/sugar-hill-housing_o.

Sumner, Jane. "Modern home broke new ground." *Austin American-Statesman*, 28 June 2009, https://www.pressreader.com/usa/austin-american-statesman-sunday/20090628/282333970890951.

Tannler, Albert M. "Louis Bellinger and the New Granada Theater." *Pittsburgh History & Landmarks Foundation*, https://phlf.org/education-department/architectural-history/articles/pittsburghs-african-american-architect-louis-bellinger-and-the-new-granada-theater/.

Tavernise, Sabrina. "A Dream Fulfilled, Martin Luther King Memorial Opens." *The New York Times*, 22 Aug. 2011, https://www.nytimes.com/2011/08/23/us/23mlk.html.

"The Temple of Jazz where the King was Crowned." *Pittsburgh Music History*, https://sites.google.com/site/pittsburghmusichistory/pittsburgh-music-story/venues/pythian-temple-savoy-ballroom.
"Theme Building, LAX." *Los Angeles Conservancy*, https://www.laconservancy.org/locations/theme-building-lax.

Tifft, Susan E. "Out of the Shadows." *Smithsonian Magazine,* 1 Feb. 2005, www.smithsonianmag.com/history/out-of-the-shadows-85569503/.

Toledano, Roulhac, et al. *New Orleans Architecture, Volume VI: Faubourg Treme and the Bayou Road ; North Rampart Street to North Broad Street, Canal Street to St. Bernard Avenue.* Pelican Pub. Co., 1980.

Trsek, Kelly. "First African Methodist Episcopal Church, Los Angeles, California, (1872-)." *Black Past*, blackpast.org/aaw/first-african-methodist-episcopal-church-1872.

Tucker, Helen A. "The Negro Building and Exhibit at the Jamestown Exposition." *Our Time Press*, 01 Dec. 2003, http://www.ourtimepress.com/the-negro-building-and-exhibit-at-the-jamestown-exposition/.
"University of Washington Ethnic Cultural Center." *University of Washington*, Jan. 2009, https://cpd.uw.edu/sites/default/files/Ethnic%20Cultural%20Center%20HRA.pdf.

"Villa Lewaro (Madam C. J. Walker Estate)." *National Trust for Historic Preservation*, https://savingplaces.org/places/villa-lewaro-madam-c-j-walker-estate#.W_DVaOhKiM-.

"Villa Lewaro National Register of Historic Places, 1976." *The Irvington Historical Society*, http://www.irvingtonhistoricalsociety.org/nrhp/nrhp04.html.

Wallace, Amy. "Plan for Schomburg Center displayed." *The New York Times*, 24 Feb. 1986, https://www.nytimes.com/1986/02/24/nyregion/plan-for-schomburg-center-displayed.html.

Walser, Lauren. "Three Influential African-American Architects You Should Know About." *National Trust for Historic Preservation*, 9 Feb. 2016, savingplaces.org/stories/three-influential-african-american-architects-you-should-know#.W-kA6JNKiM-.

"Weeksville Heritage Center, 1698-1704 Bergen Street, Brooklyn." *The New York Landmarks Conservancy*, http://www.nylandmarks.org/programs_services/grants/emergency_preservation_grants/projects/weeksville_heritage_center_1698-1704_bergen_street_brooklyn/.

"Welcome to Bienville Basin." *Bienville Basin Apartments*, https://www.bienvillebasinapartments.com/.

"What We Do." *Weeksville Heritage Center*, http://www.weeksvillesociety.org/our-vision-what-we-do/.

Whoriskey, Peter. "What happened when Brad Pitt and his architects came to rebuild New Orleans." *The Washington Post*, 28 Aug. 2015, https://www.washingtonpost.com/news/wonk/wp/2015/08/28/what-happened-when-brad-pitt-and-his-architects-came-to-rebuild-new-orleans/?noredirect=on&utm_term=.a0e7c9665359.

Williams, Clarence G. "From 'Tech' to Tuskegee: The Life of Robert Robinson Taylor, 1868-1942." *MIT*

Libraries, 13 Jan. 1998, https://libraries.mit.edu/archives/mithistory/blacks-at-mit/taylor.html.

Wilson, Lynette. "St. Philip's Church, Harlem, marks 200th anniversary." *The Episcopal Church*, 04 Oct. 2009, https://www.episcopalchurch.org/library/article/st-philips-church-harlem-marks-200th-anniversary.

Wilson, Mabel O. *Begin with the Past: Building of the National Museum of African American History and Culture*. Smithsonian Books, 2016.

Woolfolk, Odessa. "BCRI History." *Birmingham Civil Rights Institute,*

https://www.bcri.org/wp-content/uploads/2018/10/bcrihistory.pdf.

Wynn, Linda T. "McKissack and McKissack Architects (1905-)." *Tennessee State University*, ww2.tnstate.edu/library/digital/mckissack.htm.

Young, Michelle. "Inside the LAX Airport Theme Building: A Modernist Icon." *Untapped Cities*, 28 May 2013, https://untappedcities.com/2013/05/28/inside-lax-airport-theme-building-modernist-icon/.

Young, Virginia A. "Interim Development Of Hill District's

New Granada Theater Will Soon Be Underway." *90.5 WESA*, 13 Feb. 2018, http://www.wesa.fm/post/interim-development-hill-districts-new-granada-theater-will-soon-be-underway#stream/0.

Zenz, Cassandra. "Weeksville , New York (1838--)." *Black Past*, https://blackpast.org/aah/weeksville-new-york-1838.

FURTHER READING

The Directory of African American Architects. http://blackarch.uc.edu/

Gooden, Mario. *Dark Space: Architecture, Representation, Black Identity*. Columbia Books on Architecture and the City, 2016.

Kaplan, Victoria. *Structural Inequality: Black Architects in the United States*. Rowman & Littlefield, 2006.

Mitchell, Melvin L. *The Crisis of the African-American Architect: Conflicting Cul-

tures of Architecture and (Black) Power*. Writers Advantage, 2003.

Travis, Jack. *African American Architects in Current Practice*. Princeton Architectural Press, 1991.

Wilson, Dreck Spurlock. *African-American Architects: a Biographical Dictionary 1865-1945*. Routledge, 2004.

INDEX

Entries in bold and italic are Black architects.

PHOTO CREDITS

Paul Wellington works as a library supervisor and holds a Master of Architecture degree from the University of Wisconsin-Milwaukee. He enjoys LEGO architecture and has several commissioned works, including models of University of Wisconsin-Oshkosh's campus library and Unity Temple. Paul's first book is *I Love Buildings! Wisconsin*.

pawellington.com
facebook.com/pawellington
twitter.com/PAWellington00

Printed in the USA
CPSIA information can be obtained
at www.ICGtesting.com
LVHW060027141123
763606LV00060B/934